# TEACHER'S PET PUBLICATIONS

LITPLAN TEACHER PACK
for
E. A. Poe Stories
based on the stories and poems by
Edgar Allan Poe

Written by
Mary B. Collins

© 1996 Teacher's Pet Publications
All Rights Reserved

This **LitPlan** for Edgar Allan Poe's
short stories & poems
has been brought to you by Teacher's Pet Publications, Inc.

Copyright Teacher's Pet Publications 1996
11504 Hammock Point
Berlin MD 21811

Only the student materials in this unit plan (such as worksheets,
study questions, and tests) may be reproduced multiple times
for use in the purchaser's classroom.

For any additional copyright questions,
contact Teacher's Pet Publications.

www.tpet.com

TABLE OF CONTENTS - *Poe Stories*

Introduction	6
Unit Objectives	8
Reading Assignment Sheet	9
Unit Outline	10
Study Questions (Short Answer)	13
Quiz/Study Questions (Multiple Choice)	38
Pre-reading Vocabulary Worksheets	65
Lesson One (Introductory Lesson)	85
Nonfiction Assignment Sheet	87
Oral Reading Evaluation Form	89
Writing Assignment 1	108
Writing Assignment 2	116
Writing Assignment 3	119
Writing Evaluation Form	120
Vocabulary Review Activities	115
Extra Writing Assignments/Discussion ?s	112
Unit Review Activities	121
Unit Tests	125
Unit Resource Materials	155
Vocabulary Resource Materials	169

ABOUT THE AUTHOR
Edgar Allan Poe

POE, Edgar Allan (1809-49). The greatest American teller of mystery and suspense tales in the 19th century was Edgar Allan Poe. In his mysteries he invented the modern detective story. In Poe's poems, like his tales, his characters are tortured by nameless fears and longings. Today Poe is acclaimed as one of America's greatest writers, but in his own unhappy lifetime he knew little but failure.

Edgar Poe was born in Boston, Mass., on Jan. 19, 1809. His parents were touring actors. Orphaned at age 3, he was taken into the home of John Allan, a merchant of Richmond, Va. His wife reared Edgar as her son, but Allan accepted the boy largely to please her. Later Poe took Allan as his middle name, but his signature was usually Edgar A. Poe.

John Allan became one of the richest men in Virginia. He never formally adopted Poe, but the youth thought that he would be named Allan's heir. After a time, however, Allan grew cold toward him, and Poe realized that his place in the family was insecure.

When he was 17, Poe entered the University of Virginia. Allan gave Poe only a small allowance, and the young man soon began owing money. He gambled and ran into greater debt. By the end of the year he owed 2,500 dollars. He was nervous and unstable, and he began to drink. His body could not tolerate alcohol, and only a small amount made him at first intoxicated and later ill. Allan angrily withdrew Poe from school, and a few months later Poe left home.

Poe went to Boston in 1827. He persuaded a printer to issue some of his early poems in a small pamphlet. It was called 'Tamerlane and Other Poems', and the title page said simply "By a Bostonian."

Poe's money was soon gone, and he enlisted in the Army under the name of Edgar A. Perry. In his two years in the Army, he rose to be regimental sergeant major. But he wanted to become an officer, thinking that such advancement would restore him to Allan's favor. After the death of Mrs. Allan in 1829, Poe and Allan were temporarily reconciled. With Allan's help Poe was granted an honorable discharge from the Army. He then sought an appointment to the United States Military Academy at West Point, N.Y.

Poe waited for more than a year. In the meantime he lived in Baltimore, Md., with his father's widowed sister, Maria Clemm, and her young daughter, Virginia. While there he published another volume of poetry, 'Al Aaraaf, Tamerlane, and Minor Poems' (1829). On July 1, 1830, he was sworn in as a West Point cadet. He hated the discipline and the restraint of the school. When John Allan married again, Poe lost all chance of becoming his heir. He deliberately neglected his classes and duties and was expelled after eight months.

For the next four years Poe struggled to earn a living as a writer. He returned to Mrs. Clemm's home and submitted stories to magazines. His first success came in 1833, when he entered a short-story contest and won a prize of 50 dollars for the story "MS. Found in a Bottle." By 1835 he was the editor of the Southern Literary Messenger. He married his cousin Virginia, who was only 13, and Mrs. Clemm stayed with the couple. The Poes had no children.

Poe's stories, poems, and criticism in the magazine soon attracted attention, and he looked for wider opportunities. From 1837 to 1839 he tried free-lance writing in New York City and Philadelphia but earned very little. Again he tried editing (1839-42). His work was praised, but he was paid little. His efforts to organize his own magazine were unsuccessful. For the next two years he turned again to free-lance writing.

Many of his best stories were written as a regular part of his editorial work. Even those he sold for a fee rarely brought him more than 100 dollars each. Some of these were: "Narrative of Arthur Gordon Pym" (1838); "Fall of the House of Usher" (1839); "Murders in the Rue Morgue" (1843), considered the first detective story; and "The Gold Bug" (1843). During this time his wife showed symptoms of tuberculosis.

In 1844 Poe and his family moved to New York City. By now Poe was well known in literary circles, and the publication of 'The Raven and Other Poems' and 'Tales', both in 1845, enhanced his reputation. The Poes lived in a cottage in Fordham (now in the borough of the Bronx). They were comfortable for a time, but his wife soon became sicker. Poe also grew weaker and became more dissipated. During the winter of 1846-47 they had little food or fuel. Virginia Poe died on Jan. 30, 1847.

After his wife's death Poe continued to live with Mrs. Clemm in Fordham. By now he was increasingly depressed and erratic. He courted various women, in a vain attempt to find solace for the loss of his wife. In 1849 he became engaged to a childhood sweetheart, who then was a wealthy Richmond widow. After making wedding plans, he set out for New York City from Richmond but disappeared in Baltimore. He was found five days after he disappeared-drugged, intoxicated, and very near death. He died without regaining full consciousness four days later on Oct. 7, 1849.

Poe was the first American author to be widely read outside the United States. His reputation in France, especially, was enhanced by the French poet Charles Baudelaire, who read and translated Poe's works in the 1850s. Since then Poe's reputation in literature has been secure. (See Detective Story.)

--- Courtesy of Compton's Learning Company

INTRODUCTION

This unit has been designed to develop students' reading, writing, thinking, and language skills through exercises and activities related to *Poe Stories* by Edgar Allan Poe. It includes twenty lessons, supported by extra resource materials.

The **introductory lesson** introduces students to Poe's stories through a teacher-supplied pre-recorded oral presentation of *The Tell-Tale Heart* or *The Black Cat*. Students will then do the prereading work for the horror story of the teacher's choice.

This unit is set up so that the class is exposed to each of the five types of tales Poe wrote plus a selection of his poetry. The exact stories read will depend on what your school has available. On the Reading Assignment Sheet there is a note next to each tale telling what kind of a story it is. This unit is also set up so that you could use any of the stories (or the poetry) individually without doing the whole unit. Each tale has short answer study questions, multiple choice study questions, a vocabulary worksheet, and a test.

The **study guide questions** are fact-based questions; students can find the answers to these questions right in the text. These questions come in two formats: short answer or multiple choice. The best use of these materials is probably to use the short answer version of the questions as study guides for students (since answers will be more complete), and to use the multiple choice version for occasional quizzes. If your school has the appropriate equipment, it might be a good idea to make transparencies of your answer keys for the overhead projector.

The **vocabulary work** is intended to enrich students' vocabularies as well as to aid in the students' understanding of the text. Prior to each tale, students will complete a two-part worksheet for approximately 10 vocabulary words in the upcoming tale. Part I focuses on students' use of general knowledge and contextual clues by giving the sentence in which the word appears in the text. Students are then to write down what they think the words mean based on the words' usage. Part II nails down the definitions of the words by giving students dictionary definitions of the words and having students match the words to the correct definitions based on the words' contextual usage. Students should then have an understanding of the words when they meet them in the text.

After each tale, students will go back and formulate answers for the study guide questions. Discussion of these questions serves as a **review** of the most important events and ideas presented in the reading assignments.

There is a **vocabulary review** lesson which pulls together all of the fragmented vocabulary lists for the reading assignments and gives students a review of all of the words they have studied.

One lesson is devoted to the **extra discussion questions/writing assignments**. These questions focus on interpretation, critical analysis and personal response, employing a variety of thinking skills and adding to the students' understanding of the text.

There are three **writing assignments** in this unit, each with the purpose of informing, persuading, or having students express personal opinions. The first assignment is to inform: students compare and contrast the narrators of the first two stories they read. The second assignment is to express personal opinions: students write a composition in which they give their own ideas about the poem they have been assigned. The third assignment is to persuade: students write persuasive arguments convincing their audiences that Poe was, in fact, a talented writer of fiction worth reading.

In addition, there is a **nonfiction reading assignment**. Students are required to read a piece of nonfiction related in some way to *Poe Stories*. This assignment may be fulfilled through the background research students will do relating to their characters. After reading their nonfiction pieces, students will fill out a worksheet on which they answer questions regarding facts, interpretation, criticism, and personal opinions. Before and during the tale presentations, students make **oral presentations** about the nonfiction pieces they have read, giving background information and additional information to the text. This not only exposes all students to a wealth of information, it also gives students the opportunity to practice **public speaking**.

The **review lesson** pulls together all of the aspects of the unit. The teacher is given four or five choices of activities or games to use which all serve the same basic function of reviewing all of the information presented in the unit.

The **unit test** is a little different in this unit plan than in most of our others. Because this is for a group of short stories and poems, and because the teacher has a choice of which stories to use, our usual format would not work. We have included two different multiple choice test sheets for each of the short stories covered in the unit. We also have included two different multiple choice test sheets for the poetry covered in this unit. There are six different essay questions in the test section, and there are four different vocabulary tests in three different formats. The idea is that you can mix and match the test sections in any way you choose. There are no short answer unit tests in this unit. To keep the test section from becoming too unwieldy, we thought you could simply white out the multiple choice choices to make short answer tests if you preferred that format.

There are additional **support materials** included with this unit. The **resource sections** include suggestions for an in-class library, crossword and word search puzzles related to the stories, and extra vocabulary worksheets. There is a list of **bulletin board ideas** which gives the teacher suggestions for bulletin boards to go along with this unit. In addition, there is a list of **extra class activities** the teacher could choose from to enhance the unit or as a substitution for an exercise the teacher might feel is inappropriate for his/her class. **Answer keys** are located directly after the **reproducible student materials** throughout the unit. The student materials may be reproduced for use in the teacher's classroom without infringement of copyrights. No other portion of this unit may be reproduced without the written consent of Teacher's Pet Publications, Inc.

UNIT OBJECTIVES - *Poe Stories*

1. Through reading Poe's stories students will gain a better understanding of his contributions to literature; specifically, the idea of writing for an "effect" and the techniques for writing modern detective fiction.

2. Students will demonstrate their understanding of the text on four levels: factual, interpretive, critical and personal.

3. Students will be exposed to several different forms of short story tales.

4. Students will analyze Poe's poetry to gain a better understanding of the form and art of poetry.

6. Students will be given the opportunity to practice reading aloud and silently to improve their skills in each area.

7. Students will answer questions to demonstrate their knowledge and understanding of the main events and characters in *Poe Stories* as they relate to the author's theme development.

8. Students will enrich their vocabularies and improve their understanding of the stories through the vocabulary lessons prepared for use in conjunction with the stories.

9. The writing assignments in this unit are geared to several purposes:
    a. To have students demonstrate their abilities to inform, to persuade, or to express their own personal ideas
        Note: Students will demonstrate ability to write effectively to inform by developing and organizing facts to convey information. Students will demonstrate the ability to write effectively to persuade by selecting and organizing relevant information, establishing an argumentative purpose, and by designing an appropriate strategy for an identified audience. Students will demonstrate the ability to write effectively to express personal ideas by selecting a form and its appropriate elements.
    b. To check the students' reading comprehension
    c. To make students think about the ideas presented by the stories
    d. To encourage logical thinking
    e. To provide an opportunity to practice good grammar and improve students' use of the English language.

10. Students will read aloud, report, and participate in large and small group discussions to improve their public speaking and personal interaction skills.

READING ASSIGNMENT SHEET - *Poe Stories*

Date Assigned	Reading Assignment	Story Type	Completion Date
	The Tell-Tale Heart	Psychological	
	The Black Cat	Psychological	
	The Fall of the House of Usher	Gothic	
	The Purloined Letter	Detective	
	Murder in the Rue Morgue	Detective	
	The Pit and the Pendulum	Horror	
	Masque of Red Death	Horror	
	The Cask of Amontillado	Evil/Double Personality	
	The Raven	(Poem)	
	Lenore	(Poem)	
	To Helen	(Poem)	
	Ulalume	(Poem)	
	The Bells	(Poem)	
	Annabel Lee	(Poem)	

UNIT OUTLINE - *Poe Stories*

1 Introduction PV Horror	2 Study ?s Horror PV Gothic	3 Read Gothic	4 Study ?s Gothic PV Detective Poetry Assign.	5 Writing Assignment #1
6 Read Detective	7 Study?s Detective PV Psycho.	8 Read Psycho.	9 Study ?s Psycho. PV Evil/Double Personality	10 Read Amontillado
11 Study?s Amontillado Extra ?s Poe	12 Vocabulary	13 Writing Assignment #2	14 Group Activity	15 Read & Discuss Poems
16 Read & Discuss Poems	17 Nonfiction Reports	18 Writing Assignment #3	19 Review	20 Test

Key: P = Preview Study Questions   V = Vocabulary Work   R = Read

STUDY GUIDE QUESTIONS

SHORT ANSWER STUDY GUIDE QUESTIONS
The Tell-Tale Heart

1. How does Poe set the tone for the story in the first paragraph?
2. What was the relationship between the old man and the narrator?
3. Why did the narrator decide to murder the old man?
4. Using what examples does the narrator tell us he is not "mad"?
5. What is ironic about his telling us he is not "mad"?
6. "I knew what the old man felt, and pitied him, although I chuckled at heart." What did the old man feel, and what does the fact that the narrator "chuckled at heart" tell us about him?
7. What was the narrator's reaction as he gazed upon the old man's vulture eye?
8. What finally forced the narrator to leap into the room?
9. How did the narrator actually kill the old man?
10. How does the narrator get rid of the corpse?
11. Who came knocking at the door at four o'clock?
12. What was the narrator's reaction to the police?
13. In his triumph, where did the narrator place his chair while talking to the police?
14. Why did the narrator confess murdering the old man?
15. What is the climax of the story?
16. Which is more important to Poe's purpose: the murder of the old man or the description of the narrator's mental state?
17. By repeating key words and phrases, Poe controls the pace of his story, increases the tension, and emphasizes the madness of the narrator. Give several examples of Poe's use of repetition.
18. Why is the setting of The Tell-Tale Heart vague?
19. Whose heart did the narrator actually hear?

SHORT ANSWER STUDY GUIDE QUESTIONS
The Black Cat

1. In the first few paragraphs, the narrator gives us some background information about himself. What does he most stress?
2. Who was Pluto?
3. Describe the relationship between Pluto and the narrator.
4. What was the first violent act the narrator did to Pluto?
5. What second act (the narrator describes as being done in the spirit of perverseness) did he commit on Pluto?
6. On the night the narrator killed Pluto, what happened to his home?
7. Describe the second cat.
8. Describe the relationship between the second cat and the narrator.
9. What peculiar mark did the cat have?
10. Why did the narrator kill his wife?
11. How did he dispose of the body?
12. Who came on the fourth day after the murder?
13. What was the narrator's reaction to the police?
14. How did the police discover the body?
15. Where is the climax of the story?
16. Which is more important to Poe's purpose: the murders or the revealing of the narrator's mental state?
17. Why is the setting of the story vague?
18. What value does using the first person narrative add to the story?
19. "Have we not a perpetual inclination . . . to violate that which is Law, merely because we understand it to be such?" Answer Poe's rhetorical question.

STUDY GUIDE QUESTIONS
The Fall of the House of Usher

1. In what point of view is the story written?
2. How does the first paragraph set the tone?
3. Describe the house of Usher.
4. Why was the narrator going to visit Roderick Usher?
5. Describe Roderick Usher.
6. What was the diagnosis of Lady Madeline's disease?
7. What happened to Lady Madeline on the day the narrator arrived?
8. In what way(s) does "The Haunted Place" compare to Usher's house?
9. What did Usher want to do with his twin sister's body?
10. Describe the vault in which Madeline was placed.
11. What happened on the "seventh or eighth day after the placing of the Lady Madeline within the donjon"?
12. For what purpose does Poe include the details about the dark night (with dense clouds pressing upon the turrets) and the "unnatural light" which surrounded the house?
13. What happened as the narrator read the story to Roderick Usher?
14. In the third paragraph from the end of this story, Poe uses repetition again to heighten the fantastic effect in the story. Give some examples.
15. What did the living corpse of Madeline do when it came into the narrator's room?
16. What did the narrator do?
17. What happened to the House of Usher?
18. Considering the setting, characters and subject matter of The Fall of the House of Usher, explain how it is a gothic story.

STUDY GUIDE QUESTIONS
The Murders in the Rue Morgue

1. What is the purpose of Poe's discussing analytical power and ingenuity as well as chess and card games in the first four paragraphs of the story?
2. Who is Dupin?
3. How did the narrator meet Dupin, and how did they come to share the same flat?
4. What was their daily life like at the flat?
5. Dupin says, "He is a very little fellow, that's true, and would do better for the Theatre des Varieties." What do we learn about Dupin from this statement and the explanation which follows?
6. What newspaper article drew the attention of the narrator and Dupin? What was the article about?
7. What was peculiar about the murders?
8. Why was Dupin so interested in the murders?
9. Why did Dupin become involved with the case?
10. What three things confounded the police?
11. What facts that the police missed did Dupin uncover?
12. How did Dupin test his theory and lure the sailor to his apartment?
13. What "reward" did Dupin want from the sailor?
14. What series of events actually took place regarding the murders?
15. What was the reaction of the Prefect of Police to Dupin's solving the murders?
16. Poe leaves out many details by using a dash. Why does he omit the details?
17. What is the narrator's function?
18. At what point is the climax of the story? Explain.

STUDY GUIDE QUESTIONS
The Purloined Letter

1. Who was Monsieur G---, and why had he come to see Dupin and the narrator?
2. What is the problem G---- has come to discuss?
3. Who is D--- ?
4. Describe the police investigation of D---'s apartment.
5. When the Prefect returned a month later, what did Dupin give him?
6. How did Dupin get the letter?
7. Why did Dupin replace the purloined letter with a facsimile?
8. In "The Purloined Letter," the reader does not get to participate in the solving of the problem. We only get to read Dupin's account of how he solved it. Why? What is Poe trying to emphasize?
9. Again, as in many of his stories, Poe leaves out many details (such as people's names). Why?
10. G--- says, ". . . but then he is a poet, which I take to be only one remove from a fool." Why does Dupin say this reasoning by G--- helped to keep G--- from solving the problem?
11. "Perhaps it is the very simplicity of the thing which puts you at fault." What does Dupin mean?
12. ". . . occasions may occur when $x^2 + px$ is not altogether equal to q . . . ." Explain.

STUDY GUIDE QUESTIONS
The Pit and the Pendulum

1. What is the first scene the narrator describes?
2. After "swooning" and describing various states of being conscious, where does the narrator come to his senses?
3. How did the narrator first explore his dungeon?
4. In what way did he venture to explore after his first circuit? What problem did he encounter?
5. After they realized he would now cautiously avoid the pit, what fate did the narrator's captors plan for him?
6. What else was in the room with the narrator?
7. How did the narrator get free from the table under the pendulum?
8. After the narrator became free from the table, he was subjected to yet another means toward death. What was it?
9. Just as he was about to be forced into the pit, what happened?
10. One of Poe's trademarks is that he uses all of his literary tools to produce a single effect for the reader. What is the effect given by this story?
11. What effect does the ending (the narrator's being saved) have on us as readers?
12. One of Poe's favorite conflicts is that of madness vs. reason. How is that conflict resolved in his story?
13. There are many references to "hope" in this story. According to Poe, is there hope?
14. Where is the climax of this story?
15. In what ways does this story show gothic influences?

STUDY GUIDE QUESTIONS
The Masque of Red Death

1. What was The Red Death?
2. Why did Prince Prospero gather 1,000 of his subjects into his castle?
3. How many rooms were there in use the night of the masquerade ball? What were their respective colors?
4. For what did the orchestra pause each hour?
5. Why did the newly arrived masked figure draw attention?
6. What was Prince Prospero's reaction to the figure?
7. Who unmasked the figure?
8. How did the story end?
9. What is the moral of the story?
10. What single effect was Poe conveying with this story?
11. In what ways can one see a gothic influence in The Masque of Red Death?
12. Where is the climax of the story?
13. Explain the significance of Prince Prospero's name.
14. Explain the significance of "three thousand and six hundred seconds of the Time that flies."

STUDY GUIDE QUESTIONS
The Cask of Amontillado

1. Why did Montresor decide to kill Fortunato?
2. What is ironic about Fortunato's name?
3. What was Fortunato's weak point, and how did Montresor capitalize on it?
4. How does Montresor insure Fortunato will come along?
5. Why does Fortunato continue underground among the catacombs when the nitre is making his cough worse?
6. As they continue, what does Montresor offer to Fortunato? Why?
7. What "sign" of the masons did Montresor give Fortunato?
8. What did Montresor do to Fortunato when they reached the recess where the Amontillado was supposed to be?
9. Why didn't Fortunato resist?
10. How did Montresor kill Fortunato?
11. Why did Montresor's "heart grow sick"?
12. In the last portion of the story, Montresor often repeats Fortunato's words. What effect does this have?
13. What is ironic about the trowel?
14. How does Montresor have a "double personality"?
15. What is ironic about the time of the murder?
16. What gothic elements are present in this story?
17. What does the first person narrative technique add to the story?

ANSWER KEY: SHORT ANSWER STUDY QUESTIONS
Poe Stories

The Tell-Tale Heart

1. How does Poe set the tone for the story in the first paragraph?
    The narrator introduces the idea that we think he is "mad." Poe uses the repetition of words and rhythms in his sentences which project nervousness and have the effect of building tension.

2. What was the relationship between the old man and the narrator?
    The narrator said, "I loved the old man. He had never wronged me. He had given me no insult."

3. Why did the narrator decide to murder the old man?
    He didn't like the old man's "vulture eye."

4. Using what examples does the narrator tell us he is not "mad"?
    He continually tells us how wisely, how cautiously he proceeded, how careful he was in committing the murder. He describes his patience when entering the room, and the precautions he took concealing the body.

5. What is ironic about his telling us he is not "mad"?
    The more he tells us he is not mad, the more obvious it becomes to us, the readers, that he IS mad.

6. "I knew what the old man felt, and pitied him, although I chuckled at heart." What did the old man feel, and what does the fact that the narrator "chuckled at heart" tell us about him?
    He felt fear, hearing and sensing another presence in his bedroom. The narrator truly is mad, taking delight in another man's fear.

7. What was the narrator's reaction as he gazed upon the old man's vulture eye?
    It made him furious.

8. What finally forced the narrator to leap into the room?
    He couldn't stand the beating of the heart; he thought someone might hear.

9. How did the narrator actually kill the old man?
    He pulled the bed over him and suffocated him.

10. How does the narrator get rid of the corpse?
    He dismembers it and puts it under the floor boards.

11. Who came knocking at the door at four o'clock?
    The police came, responding to a call of a neighbor who had heard a scream.

12. What was the narrator's reaction to the police?
    He was calm and greeted them warmly. He explained that he had cried out in his sleep and that the old man was away in the country. Then, he became overconfident and invited them in, showed them the house and invited them to sit.

13. In his triumph, where did the narrator place his chair while talking to the police?
    He placed his chair right over the floor boards where the old man's body was hidden.

14. Why did the narrator confess murdering the old man?
    He couldn't stand hearing the beating of the heart. The police seemed not to hear it, but as it grew louder and louder, the narrator's confidence vanished and he had to confess.

15. What is the climax of the story?
    The narrator's confession is the climax.

16. Which is more important to Poe's purpose: the murder of the old man or the description of the narrator's mental state?
    The revelation of the narrator's mental state is more important. The murder is just one incident, the reason why we are able to examine the workings of the narrator's mind.

17. By repeating key words and phrases, Poe controls the pace of his story, increases the tension, and emphasizes the madness of the narrator. Give several examples of Poe's use of repetition.
    Some examples are: very, very dreadfully nervous; not destroyed, not dulled; all closed, closed; slowly -- very, very slowly; cautiously -- oh, so cautiously -- cautiously. There are more examples; these are just a few.

18. Why is the setting of The Tell-Tale Heart vague?
    The setting doesn't really matter; what is important to Poe is the examination of the narrator's mind. Also, it allows the reader to immerse himself in the story using his own imagination and therefore more fully sensing the effect of the story.

19. Whose heart did the narrator actually hear?
    He actually heard his own heart.

ANSWER KEY: SHORT ANSWER STUDY QUESTIONS - *The Black Cat*

1. In the first few paragraphs, the narrator gives us some background information about himself. What does he most stress?
    He stresses that he is not mad, that he is a common, ordinary, mild-mannered individual capable of reason. Since the events of this story, he has become irrational and excitable.

2. Who was Pluto?
    Pluto is the narrator's cat.

3. Describe the relationship between Pluto and the narrator.
    At first, they are very close; the narrator is very fond of the cat. Then, because the narrator has a bit of an alcohol problem, the relationship changes.

4. What was the first violent act the narrator did to Pluto?
    He cut the cat's eye out.

5. What second act (the narrator describes as being done in the spirit of perverseness) did he commit on Pluto?
    He hanged the cat by a rope from a tree and killed it.

6. On the night the narrator killed Pluto, what happened to his home?
    His house burned down leaving only one wall with a figure of a cat with a rope around its neck.

7. Describe the second cat.
    The second cat looked very much like Pluto except it had a white mark on its neck.

8. Describe the relationship between the second cat and the narrator.
    At first the narrator liked it and was kind to it, but he grew to dislike it and eventually hated it. He would have killed it, but he feared it.

9. What peculiar mark did the cat have?
    He had some white on his neck/breast area. The narrator began to think it looked like gallows.

10. Why did the narrator kill his wife?
    He just about tripped over the cat and was ready to kill it with an axe when his wife grabbed his arm and stopped him. Instead of killing the cat, in his rage, he killed his wife.

11. How did he dispose of the body?
    He bricked her up in a false chimney wall.

12. Who came on the fourth day after the murder?
    The police arrived.

13. What was the narrator's reaction to the police?
    He invited them in -- even took them to the basement.

14. How did the police discover the body?
    In his over-confidence, the narrator hit the wall behind which was the body. The cat screamed from within, giving away the hiding place.

15. Where is the climax of the story?
    The climax of the story is when the cat screams from behind the wall informing the police about the narrator's murdering his wife.

16. Which is more important to Poe's purpose: the murders or the revealing of the narrator's mental state?
    The murders are just the events by which we are allowed to examine the narrator's mind. Examining the narrator's mental state is most important.

17. Why is the setting of the story vague?
    The setting is not very important to the story; it is a story of psychology. It is also a story of effect. Because the reader has to use his/her imagination to fill in any gaps Poe leaves, he becomes more immersed in the story and the effect of the story will be greater.

18. What value does using the first person narrative add to the story?
    It allows us to see the workings of the narrator's mind and it also makes us closer to the story (thus making the effect of the story greater).

19. "Have we not a perpetual inclination . . . to violate that which is Law, merely because we understand it to be such?" Answer Poe's rhetorical question.
    (The answer here is a matter of opinion. The purpose of the question is just to get students to think -- to form an opinion about a question.)

ANSWER KEY: SHORT ANSWER STUDY QUESTIONS - *The Fall of the House of Usher*

1. In what point of view is the story written?
    The story is written in the first person.

2. How does the first paragraph set the tone?
    Words like "dull," "dark," "gloomy," and "dreary" give a sense of evil. The narrator is alone; that makes us think of how we would feel if we were alone in such a place (begins to build suspense).

3. Describe the house of Usher.
    The house of Usher is an old mansion with all the gothic trappings. It is "melancholy," "bleak," "sorrowful," and has "vacant and eye-like windows." The narrator speaks about the icy feeling the house gives him.

4. Why was the narrator going to visit Roderick Usher?
    Usher had written a note to his old schoolmate (the narrator) asking him to come because he, the narrator, had been ill of late and wished to have his friend's company for cheer.

5. Describe Roderick Usher.
    He had "a cadaverousness of complexion; an eye large, liquid and luminous beyond comparison; lips somewhat thin and very pallid, . . . a finely moulded chin, . . . and hair of a more than web-like softness and tenuity."

6. What was the diagnosis of Lady Madeline's disease?
    "A settled apathy, a gradual wasting away of the person, and frequent although transient affections of a partially cataleptical character were the unusual diagnosis."

7. What happened to Lady Madeline on the day the narrator arrived?
    She "succumbed to her disease."

8. In what way(s) does "The Haunted Place" compare to Usher's house?
    Both houses are old with far better (happier) days gone by. Both have come to have some "evil things" within their walls.

9. What did Usher want to do with his twin sister's body?
    He wanted to place it in a vault within the house for a fortnight.

10. Describe the vault in which Madeline was placed.
    It was small, damp, dark, beneath the narrator's room, sheathed with copper, and it had a massive iron door.

11. What happened on the "seventh or eighth day after the placing of the Lady Madeline within the donjon"?
    The narrator felt a sense of nervousness, horror and fear.

12. For what purpose does Poe include the details about the dark night (with dense clouds pressing upon the turrets) and the "unnatural light" which surrounded the house?
    These details add to the gothic atmosphere of terror and suspense.

13. What happened as the narrator read the story to Roderick Usher?
    As he read, parts of the book seemed to become "real." He heard a cracking and ripping sound, screaming or a grating sound, and a ringing or metallic reverberation.

14. In the third paragraph from the end of this story, Poe uses repetition again to heighten the fantastic effect in the story. Give some examples.
    Some examples are: Long -- long -- long -- many minutes, many hours, many days; I dared not -- I dared not; and many, many days ago. See the paragraph referenced for more examples.

15. What did the living corpse of Madeline do when it came into the narrator's room?
    It fell on Roderick.

16. What did the narrator do?
    He fled!

17. What happened to the House of Usher?
    It cracked and fell into pieces into the tarn.

18. Considering the setting, characters and subject matter of *The Fall of the House of Usher*, explain how it is a gothic story.
    It is set in an old house (castle-like) full of rooms. It is dark inside with tombs beneath/within. The outdoors, when described, are dark, cloudy, threatening. There is a sensitive, eccentric hero. Also, there is a living corpse -- death-like in life and life-like in death.

ANSWER KEY: SHORT ANSWER STUDY QUESTIONS - *The Murders in the Rue Morgue*

1. What is the purpose of Poe's discussing analytical power and ingenuity as well as chess and card games in the first four paragraphs of the story?
    Poe's stories of detective fiction dealt with the analytical mind, the reasoning, intellectual mind of his detective (Dupin). It is his ability to observe details and analyze them rationally (and with an open-mind enough to not rule out any solution) which gives him the power to solve mysteries others cannot. In these first few pages, a philosophy of sorts is set out to prepare the reader for the methods of the "detective" Dupin.

2. Who is Dupin?
    Dupin is a man of good background. Although his family fortune has been lost, enough remains for him to live economically. His interests are intellectual. He doesn't go out often, and his sole luxury is buying books. He is the "detective" of the story.

3. How did the narrator meet Dupin, and how did they come to share the same flat?
    They met at the library, where they were both looking for the same rare book. After some time, seeing they had common interests, they decided to share expenses and live at the same flat.

4. What was their daily life like at the flat?
    Dupin was "enamored of the night." "At first dawn . . . we closed all the (inside) shutters of our old building, ignited a couple of tapers. . . ." They spent their days reading, writing, and conversing. In the evening, they went walking in the streets continuing the discussions they'd had during the day.

5. Dupin says, "He is a very little fellow, that's true, and would do better for the Theatre des Varieties." What do we learn about Dupin from this statement and the explanation which follows?
    Dupin has an acute eye for observing details and a very logical, analytical mind.

6. What newspaper article drew the attention of the narrator and Dupin? What was the article about?
    It was about murders which had taken place in the Rue (Street) Morgue. Namely, Madame L'Espanaye and Mademoiselle Camille L'Espanaye had been brutally murdered.

7. What was peculiar about the murders?
    The apartment was in disarray; Madame L'Espanaye was found head-downward up the chimney; the old lady had her throat cut so badly that the head fell off when the body was moved, and she was "fearfully mutilated." The witnesses said they could discern the voice of a Frenchman, but no one could agree on the nationality of the second voice they heard. There were four thousand francs in gold left in the room. There was no visible means of egress for the murderer(s).

8. Why was Dupin so interested in the murders?
   Being of an analytical mind and intellectually curious, the murders intrigued him.

9. Why did Dupin become involved with the case?
   The person accused of the murders, Le Bon, "once rendered [him] a service for which [he was] not ungrateful."

10. What three things confounded the police?
    a. The absence of a means of escape
    b. The seeming impossibility of reconciling the voices they heard
    c. The absence of motive for the brutal murders

11. What facts that the police missed did Dupin uncover?
    a. That one window only appeared to be nailed shut (and was thus a means of entry and escape)
    b. The intruder had to be agile to get from the window to the lightning-rod
    c. The marks on Mademoiselle L'Espanaye's neck matched those of an Ourang-Outang's hands
    d. The hair Madame L'Espanaye clutched was not human
    e. There was a small piece of ribbon he thought to be from a sailor's hair, tied with a knot particular to the Maltese

12. How did Dupin test his theory and lure the sailor to his apartment?
    He placed an ad in the paper looking for the owner of an Ourang-Outang.

13. What "reward" did Dupin want from the sailor?
    He wanted all the information about the murders in the Rue Morgue.

14. What series of events actually took place regarding the murders?
    The sailor's Ourang-Outang watched him shave and escaped with a razor. He saw the lighted window, climbed up to it and went in. In trying to imitate shaving, he got carried away and slit Madame L'Espanaye's throat. The blood frightened him; he grabbed and strangled the girl in his frenzy. He realized he did something wrong and tried to conceal the bodies -- one up the chimney and one out the window. The Frenchman (having followed the beast) ran for home. The Ourang-Outang left through the window (when it heard voices coming up the stairs) and apparently closed the window behind it.

15. What was the reaction of the Prefect of Police to Dupin's solving the murders?
    He "could not conceal his chagrin at the turn which affairs had taken," and wished Dupin would mind his own business. He was neither happy nor grateful.

16. Poe leaves out many details by using a dash. Why does he omit the details?
    The exact time and people's names are not important; he wishes to show the events, the relationships, the uncovering of the facts. Also, using non-specific language regarding certain facts, Poe allows the reader to become more involved.

17. What is the narrator's function?
    He is our eyes into the mystery; he is very much like us in that he can only deduce what the average reader can deduce. Also, he gives the main character, Dupin, someone to interact with and explain things to so we, too, can see and understand the brilliant solutions and how they come about.

18. At what point is the climax of the story? Explain.
    The climax is at the point when the sailor is confronted with providing an explanation for the murders; it is then that Dupin's theory is tested and we find out whether or not he has reasoned correctly.

ANSWER KEY: SHORT ANSWER STUDY QUESTIONS - *The Purloined Letter*

1. Who was Monsieur G---, and why had he come to see Dupin and the narrator?
    G--- was the Prefect of Police. He had come to see Dupin about a police matter.

2. What is the problem G---- has come to discuss?
    ". . . a certain document of the most importance has been purloined from the royal apartments. . . . The individual who purloined it is known. . . . The disclosure of the documents to a third person . . . would bring in question the honor of a personage of most exalted station; and this fact gives the holder of the document an ascendancy over the . . . personage whose honor and peace are jeopardized."

3. Who is D--- ?
    D--- is the person who has stolen the letter.

4. Describe the police investigation of D---'s apartment.
    The police have looked at it -- every minute inch of it -- and have even used a microscope, looking for any tiny detail which might lead to a clue as to the whereabouts of the letter.

5. When the Prefect returned a month later, what did Dupin give him?
    He had the purloined letter.

6. How did Dupin get the letter?
    He went to visit D--- , wearing dark glasses so D--- couldn't see him looking around the room. He noticed a letter which he deduced was the purloined letter. He made a mental note of the letter's appearance. He left his snuff box at D---'s place, so he could return the next day with a replica of the purloined letter. He pre-arranged a diversion on the second day, and switched the letters, recovering the purloined letter.

7. Why did Dupin replace the purloined letter with a facsimile?
    He did not want D--- to suspect the loss of the letter until after he (Dupin) had left. Also, he is helping to cause the political ruin of D--- as revenge on behalf of the lady involved.

8. In "The Purloined Letter," the reader does not get to participate in the solving of the problem. We only get to read Dupin's account of how he solved it. Why? What is Poe trying to emphasize?
    He is trying to emphasize the method of Dupin's solution -- the use of logic and reasoning in solving a mystery.

9. Again, as in many of his stories, Poe leaves out many details (such as people's names). Why?
    The names are not important; the method of solution is the thing Poe wished to emphasize.

10. G--- says, ". . . but then he is a poet, which I take to be only one remove from a fool." Why does Dupin say this reasoning by G--- helped to keep G--- from solving the problem?
    G--- underestimated D---. Dupin knew D--- to be "both a mathematician and a poet" and thus was aware of D---'s ability to use logic and reason.

11. "Perhaps it is the very simplicity of the thing which puts you at fault." What does Dupin mean?
    The detectives were so busy looking for some small clue as to where a particularly described letter would be, that they missed the obvious clues. The police were methodically looking for a thing; Dupin considered the person and his motives and the psychology of the situation to find the obvious.

12. ". . . occasions may occur when $x^2 + px$ is not altogether equal to q . . . ." Explain.
    If in working out a problem you predispose yourself to a certain solution, other solutions don't seem possible. Things aren't always as they appear to be. Keep an open mind that there may be exceptions to the formula, the rule, the accepted train of thought.

ANSWER KEY: SHORT ANSWER STUDY QUESTIONS - *The Pit and the Pendulum*

1. What is the first scene the narrator describes?
    He describes the courtroom scene when he was sentenced to death.

2. After "swooning" and describing various states of being conscious, where does the narrator come to his senses?
    He finds himself in a pitch-dark dungeon.

3. How did the narrator first explore his dungeon?
    He found a wall, placed a piece of cloth at a right angle from the wall on the floor (to mark his beginning point) and proceeded to follow the wall (until he fell asleep).

4. In what way did he venture to explore after his first circuit? What problem did he encounter?
    He decided to cross the room in a direct line. He fell on his face and discovered the pit.

5. After they realized he would now cautiously avoid the pit, what fate did the narrator's captors plan for him?
    They tied him to a table over which a razor-sharp, steel crescent slowly descended in the motion of a clock pendulum. They intended for him to be repeatedly sliced and for him to bleed to death.

6. What else was in the room with the narrator?
    Rats were in the room.

7. How did the narrator get free from the table under the pendulum?
    He wiped his food over the parts of the ropes he could reach so the rats would eat through them.

8. After the narrator became free from the table, he was subjected to yet another means toward death. What was it?
    The walls of the room began to move inward, pushing him towards the pit.

9. Just as he was about to be forced into the pit, what happened?
    The walls stopped. He was saved; the Inquisition was over.

10. One of Poe's trademarks is that he uses all of his literary tools to produce a single effect for the reader. What is the effect given by this story?
    The effect is the feeling of terror -- the fear of inevitable death.

11. What effect does the ending (the narrator's being saved) have on us as readers?
    It is one of surprise and relief.

12. One of Poe's favorite conflicts is that of madness vs. reason. How is that conflict resolved in this story?
    Reason wins.

13. There are many references to "hope" in this story. According to Poe, is there hope?
    The narrator feels hopeful until the end (although he goes through periods of hopelessness). The ending would suggest that Poe does think there is always hope -- whether rational solutions are within our power or not; outside forces could intervene.

14. Where is the climax of this story?
    The climax is at the very end as he is about to finally be pushed into the pit.

15. In what ways does this story show gothic influences?
    The story has several gothic elements: a dark chamber (dungeon) presumably in some larger castle-like building, grotesque torture, struggle between life/consciousness and death/unconsciousness, and a feeling of fear and terror.

ANSWER KEY: SHORT ANSWER STUDY QUESTIONS - *The Masque of Red Death*

1. What was The Red Death?
    It was a highly contagious disease.

2. Why did Prince Prospero gather 1,000 of his subjects into his castle?
    He wanted to save those in his kingdom who had not yet contracted the disease.

3. How many rooms were there in use the night of the masquerade ball? What were their respective colors?
    There were seven rooms: the blue room (eastern), the purple room, the green room, the orange room, the white room, the violet room and the black (western) room.

4. For what did the orchestra pause each hour?
    They paused for the striking of the ebony clock.

5. Why did the newly arrived masked figure draw attention?
    All of the costumes were grotesque, but this one was so horrid everyone stopped to look. It was dressed as a corpse of a person who had died of the Red Death.

6. What was Prince Prospero's reaction to the figure?
    He bellowed that someone should unmask this one who had given such an insult as to dress as the dreaded Red Death.

7. Who unmasked the figure?
    No one was brave enough to touch it. However, when they went into the black room, they realized that no tangible form inhabited the costume.

8. How did the story end?
    Everyone in the black room contracted the disease and died.

9. What is the moral of the story?
    You can't hide from death.

10. What single effect was Poe conveying with this story?
    He was conveying horror.

11. In what ways can one see a gothic influence in The Masque of Red Death?
    There are many gothic influences: a castle, darkness, long ago/far away, and the crossing over of life/death.

12. Where is the climax of the story?
    The climax was when the people realized that Red Death had come.

13. Explain the significance of Prince Prospero's name.
    Prospero is a play on "prosperous." He is ironically a prince without prosperity, without life or a kingdom at the end of the party.

14. Explain the significance of "three thousand and six hundred seconds of the Time that flies."
    This line emphasizes the fleeting moments of life slipping by.

ANSWER KEY: SHORT ANSWER STUDY QUESTIONS - *The Cask of Amontillado*

1. Why did Montresor decide to kill Fortunato?
    "The thousand injuries of Fortunato I had borne as I best could; but when he ventured upon insult, I vowed revenge."

2. What is ironic about Fortunato's name?
    He is not fortunate at all.

3. What was Fortunato's weak point, and how did Montresor capitalize on it?
    Fortunato loved wines and considered himself a great connoisseur. Montresor invited him to help identify his rare Amontillado wine.

4. How does Montresor insure Fortunato will come along?
    He insinuates that Luchesi can test it for him since Fortunato seems busy. Montresor knows Fortunato won't miss a chance to taste the rare wine and prove his connoisseurship.

5. Why does Fortunato continue underground among the catacombs when the nitre is making his cough worse?
    Montresor invites Fortunato to stop and turn back but he mentions that Luchesi could help him instead. He knows that Fortunato's pride will keep him going.

6. As they continue, what does Montresor offer to Fortunato? Why?
    He offers him wine. He says it will "defend them from the damps." Actually, he is getting Fortunato drunk.

7. What "sign" of the masons did Montresor give Fortunato?
    He showed a trowel.

8. What did Montresor do to Fortunato when they reached the recess where the Amontillado was supposed to be?
    He followed him and chained him to a granite wall.

9. Why didn't Fortunato resist?
    He was dumbfounded and drunk.

10. How did Montresor kill Fortunato?
    He bricked-up the recess so there was no hope of escape for Fortunato, and he allowed the nitre and natural causes to do the rest.

11. Why did Montresor's "heart grow sick"?
    "On account of the dampness in the catacombs" (not because of the murder).

12. In the last portion of the story, Montresor often repeats Fortunato's words. What effect does this have?
    It shows his cold heartedness -- perhaps his madness. We know Montresor says the same words with a different tone.

13. What is ironic about the trowel?
    It is a sign of the Masons and Montresor uses it to wall-in Fortunato just after Fortunato claims Montresor is not good enough to be a Mason. (Actually, Montresor is a very good "mason.")

14. How does Montresor have a "double personality"?
    He shows one side, an ordinary, friendly, rational side, to Fortunato. But, he has another side which is mad/irrational which we see towards the end of the story.

15. What is ironic about the time of the murder?
    It is carnival time, a happy time when one would not expect such a bizarre murder.

16. What gothic elements are present in this story?
    There are many gothic elements: catacombs/bodies, large old mansion, distant time, life/death.

17. What does the first person narrative technique add to the story?
    It helps to get the reader involved. We don't get any information except that from the mind of the narrator (however perverse that may be!) It also helps create suspense.

STUDY GUIDE/QUIZ QUESTIONS - *Poe Stories*
Multiple Choice Format

The Tell-Tale Heart

1. How does Poe set the tone for the story in the first paragraph?
    A. He uses repetition of words and rhythms to introduce the idea that the narrator is mad.
    B. He uses reference to hell to show that the narrator is evil.
    C. He uses references to disease to portray the narrator as sickly.
    D. He uses questions to show that the narrator is insecure.

2. What was the relationship between the old man and the narrator?
    A. The narrator hated the man.
    B. The narrator didn't know the man; he had been hired to do the killing.
    C. The narrator loved the man.
    D. They had been business partners, but the old man cheated the narrator. Now he wanted to get even.

3. Why did the narrator decide to murder the old man?
    A. He wanted to steal the old man's fortune.
    B. He thought he heard the voice of the devil telling him to do it.
    C. He was afraid the old man would kill him if he had a chance.
    D. He didn't like the old man's eye; it reminded him of a vulture.

4. The narrator uses several examples to tell us he is not mad. Which of these is not one of the examples?
    A. He proceeded wisely and cautiously.
    B. He made sure he wore black clothes.
    C. He was patient when entering the room.
    D. He took precautions to conceal the body.

5. The more the author tells us he is not mad, the more obvious it becomes to us, the readers, that he is mad. Of what literary device is this an example?
    A. Foreshadowing
    B. Personification
    C. Irony
    D. Alliteration

6. "I knew what the old man felt, and pitied him, although I chuckled at heart." What did the old man feel?
    A. He felt fear at hearing and sensing another person in his bedroom.
    B. He felt lonely, because there was no one to call for help.
    C. He felt old, realizing that he could not hear or see well.
    D. He felt tired and dizzy because he had been awakened from a sound sleep.

7. Why did the narrator "chuckle at heart?"
    A. He had a good sense of humor.
    B. He laughed silently so as not to make noise.
    C. He was truly mad, taking delight in another man's fear.
    D. He was really nervous, and chuckling relieved his tension.

Tell Tale Heart Multiple Choice Study Questions page 2

8. What was the narrator's reaction as he gazed upon the old man's vulture eye?
    A. It mad him sad.
    B. It made him nostalgic.
    C. It made him tranquil.
    D. It made him furious.

9. What finally forced the narrator to leap into the room?
    A. He thought he heard the man getting out of bed and coming towards the door.
    B. He couldn't stand the beating of the heart; he thought someone might hear.
    C. His lantern was running our of fuel.
    D. He heard footsteps in the corridor, and thought someone was coming.

10. How did the narrator actually kill the old man?
    A. He drove a knife through his eye and into his brain.
    B. He shot him.
    C. He hit him over the head with the lantern.
    D. He pulled the bed over and suffocated him.

11. How does the narrator get rid of the corpse?
    A. He dismembers it and puts it under the floorboards.
    B. He burns it in the house's furnace.
    C. He stuffs it in an old trunk.
    D. He leaves it outside for the animals to destroy.

12. What happened at four o'clock?
    A. There was a violent thunderstorm. The narrator thought it was an omen.
    B. The housekeeper came upstairs to check on the old man.
    C. The police came in response to a call from a neighbor.
    D. The narrator realized what he had done and turned himself in.

13. What was the narrator's reaction to the police?
    A. He was afraid, and acted nervous. He told them the old man had a contagious disease and couldn't be seen.
    B. He was angry. he silently vowed to get rid of the neighbor who had called them. He let the police in but did not talk to them.
    C. He was calm and greeted them warmly. He invited them in to chat.
    D. He was cautious. He pretended that he didn't understand what they wanted. He thought they would leave if they thought he was slow-witted.

14. In his triumph, what did the narrator do while talking to the police?
    A. He sat on the bed he had used to smother the man.
    B. He placed his chair right over the floor boards where the body was hidden.
    C. He wore the old man's dressing gown.
    D. He told them stories about how cruel and strange the old man was.

15. Why did the narrator confess to murdering the old man?
    A. He couldn't stand the beating of the heart.
    B. The police found the tub where he had collected the blood.
    C. He thought he say the old man's ghost in the doorway.
    D. He thought they would be easier on him if he confessed.

Tell Tale Heart Multiple Choice Study Questions page 3

16. What is the climax of the story?
    A. The old man's death is the climax.
    B. The arrival of the police is the climax.
    C. Burying the body is the climax.
    D. The narrator's confession is the climax.

17. Which is most important to Poe's purpose?
    A. The murder of the old man is most important.
    B. The description of the narrator's mental state is most important.
    C. The arrival of the police is most important.
    D. The night-time setting is most important.

18. By repeating key words and phrases, Poe controls the pace of the story, increases the tension, and emphasizes the madness of the narrator. Which of these is not an example of Poe's use of repetition?
    A. For an hour, a whole hour
    B. Slowly-very slowly
    C. Cautiously--oh, so cautiously
    D. Very, very dreadfully nervous

19. Why is the setting of the Tell-Tale Heart vague?
    A. It is based on a true story and Poe didn't want the actual people involved to realize he was writing about them.
    B. Poe is not really very good at developing settings.
    C. The examination of the narrator's mind is most important to Poe.
    D. Poe wants the reader to realize that this could happen to anyone.

20. What did the narrator actually hear?
    A. He heard the man's pocket watch.
    B. He heard his own heart beating.
    C. He heard the floor boards creaking.
    D. He heard one of the policemen tapping his foot.

MULTIPLE CHOICE STUDY QUESTIONS - *The Black Cat*

1. In the first few paragraphs, the narrator gives us some background information about himself. What does he most stress?
    A. He stresses that he has been suffering for a long time from depression, and that he is under a doctor's care.
    B. He stresses that he is a very religious person who makes decisions only after reading the Bible and consulting with his clergyman.
    C. He stresses that he is not mad, but has recently become irrational and excitable.
    D. He stresses that he had been badly scared by an animal when he was young, and had been trying ever since to become comfortable in their presence.

2. Who is Pluto?
    A. Pluto is the narrator's cat.
    B. Pluto is the narrator's dog.
    C. Pluto is the narrator's doctor.
    D. Pluto is the barkeep in the narrator's favorite tavern.

3. Describe the relationship between Pluto and the narrator.
    A. They do not like each other, and antagonize one another whenever they are together.
    B. The narrator likes Pluto, but Pluto prefers the company of the narrator's wife, which causes him to become jealous.
    C. They remain great friends throughout the story.
    D. At first they are very close. The relationship changes later because of the narrator's alcohol problem.

4. What was the first violent act the narrator did to Pluto?
    A. He broke Pluto's leg.
    B. He cut Pluto's eye out.
    C. He threw Pluto in the icy river.
    D. He starved Pluto for two weeks.

5. What second act did the narrator commit on Pluto?
    A. He cut off his ears.
    B. He hung Pluto from a rope and killed him.
    C. He buried Pluto alive in the yard.
    D. He threw Pluto into the fire place and burned him.

6. What was left of the narrator's home after the fire?
    A. The tree in the garden was the only thing left.
    B. The narrator's bed was the only thing left.
    C. One wall with the figure of a cat on it was left.
    D. The cat's body was left, lying on the charred remains of the mattress.

7. Describe the second cat.
    A. The second cat was the opposite of Pluto; it was all white.
    B. The second cat was the same color as Pluto, but it had two eyes.
    C. The second cat was larger than Pluto, and had black fur and white paws.
    D. The second cat looked a lot like Pluto, but it had a white mark on its neck.

The Black Cat Multiple Choice Study Questions page 2

8. Described the relationship between the second cat and the narrator.
   A. At first he liked it, but soon grew to hate it. He was afraid of it, so he didn't kill it.
   B. The narrator liked the cat, but the cat was nasty and ill-tempered around him. He tried to get rid of it, but the cat kept returning.
   C. The cat didn't like the narrator, and tries several times to run away. The narrator kept the cat in a cage so it couldn't escape.
   D. The narrator and the cat liked each other at first. Soon the narrator's wife became jealous of all of the attention the narrator gave the cat, and wanted him to get rid of it. The narrator refused.

9. What peculiar mark did the cat have?
   A. The cat had a white circle around one eye. It reminded the narrator of the first cat's missing eye.
   B. The cat had a white mark on its back. The narrator thought it looked like his initials.
   C. The cat had white streaks on its face that reminded the narrator of drops of blood.
   D. The cat had some white on its neck/breast area. The narrator thought it looked like gallows.

10. Why did the narrator kill his wife?
    A. He was delirious and thought she was turning into a cat.
    B. She tried to stop him from killing the cat. He killed her in his rage.
    C. She wanted to get rid of the cat. She told him she would leave if he kept the cat. He meant to scare her, and accidentally killed her.
    D. He thought he heard the voice of the first cat telling him to do it.

11. How did he dispose of the body?
    A. He cut it up and burned it.
    B. He dug a grave and buried it in the floor of the cellar.
    C. He bricked it up in the chimney wall.
    D. He packed it in a box, took it out of the house, and threw it in the river.

12. Who came on the fourth day after the murder?
    A. His in-laws came.
    B. The neighbors came.
    C. The police came.
    D. The doctor and nurse came.

13. What was the narrator's reaction to the arrival?
    A. He told them his wife was away on a trip, and wouldn't let them in.
    B. He said he was sick, and asked them not to stay too long.
    C. He pretended he wasn't home, and didn't let them in.
    D. He invited them in and showed them around the house.

14. How did the police discover the body?
    A. The stench from the decaying body was overwhelming. The police were able to find the body by tracing the smell.
    B. The narrator hit the wall that covered the body. The cat screamed from within.
    C. One of the policemen leaned against the wall. The wet plaster rubbed off onto his coat, causing the police to inspect the wall more closely.
    D. The cat came into the room and began clawing and scratching at the wall. The narrator tried to move it, but by then the police were suspicious.

The Black Cat Multiple Choice Study Questions page 3

15. Where is the climax of the story?
    A. The climax is when the narrator kills his wife.
    B. The climax is when the narrator finds the second cat.
    C. The climax is when the cat screams.
    D. The climax is when the narrator is hung.

16. Which of these is the most important to Poe's purpose?
    A. Examining the narrator's mental state.
    B. Showing cruelty to animals.
    C. Surprising the reader.
    D. Describing the murders.

17. How does Poe allow the reader to become more immersed in the story?
    A. He names the cats but not the wife.
    B. He describes things in great detail.
    C. He keeps the cat's entombment a secret.
    D. He uses vague setting.

18. What value does using the first person narrative add to the story?
    A. It allows us to see the workings of the mind of the narrator.
    B. It makes the action go more quickly.
    C. It eliminates unnecessary characters.
    D. It makes the story easier to follow.

MULTIPLE CHOICE STUDY QUESTIONS - *The Fall of the House of Usher*

1. In what point of view is the story written?
    A. The story is written in third person.
    B. The story is written in second person.
    C. The story is written in third person, omniscient author.
    D. The story is written in first person.

2. Which of these is not used to set the tone in the first paragraph?
    A. Words like "dark," "dull," "gloomy," and "dreary" give a sense of evil.
    B. The narrator alludes to his own madness.
    C. He is alone, which makes us think of how we would feel if we were alone in such a place.
    D. The narrator refers to the house as a "mystery."

3. Which of these sentences describes the House of Usher?
    A. It looks like a medieval castle, complete with a moat and a drawbridge.
    B. It is a modern, one story building that sprawls over the grounds.
    C. It is an old mansion with all of the gothic trappings.
    D. It is a Tudor style manor house, rather worn down.

4. Why was the narrator going to visit Roderick Usher?
    A. They were old schoolmates. Usher wanted his friend's company while he recuperated from an illness.
    B. They were long-lost brothers, who had just been reunited. They wanted to take some time to get to know each other.
    C. The narrator was a student who was going to rent rooms from Usher while he studied.
    D. The narrator was a doctor. He had offered to treat Usher for free if Usher would agree to use a new technique the doctor had developed.

5. Which of these phrases does not describe Roderick Usher?
    A. A cadaverousness of complexion
    B. Thick, curly, wiry hair
    C. Thin, pallid lips
    D. Large, liquid, luminous eyes

6. What was the diagnosis of Lady Madeline's disease?
    A. She had leprosy.
    B. She had cerebral palsy.
    C. She had acute rhinitis and meningitis.
    D. She had a partially cataleptical character and a settled apathy.

7. What happened to Lady Madeline on the day the narrator arrived?
    A. She died.
    B. She was miraculously cured.
    C. She retired to her room and never came out again.
    D. She fell in love with him.

8. In what ways does "The Haunted Palace" compare to Usher's house?
    A. Both are the same size.
    B. Both were built at the same time, with the same type of materials.
    C. Both are old and have some evil things within their walls.
    D. Both were owned by the Usher family.

Fall of the House of Usher Multiple Choice Study Questions page 2

9. What did Usher want to do with his twin sister's body?
    A. He wanted to bury it in the yard under her favorite tree.
    B. He wanted to take it to the church cemetery immediately.
    C. He wanted to preserve it by leaving it in her room.
    D. He wanted to place it in a vault within the house for a fortnight.

10. Describe the vault in which Madeline was placed.
    A. It was small, damp, and dark. It was sheathed with copper and had a massive iron door.
    B. It was large and airy. It had marble floors and rich tapestries hung on the walls.
    C. It wasn't much bigger than a safe, and was made of iron, with a steel door.
    D. It was made of the finest mahogany with an oak door.

11. What happened on the "seventh or eighth day after the placing of the Lady Madeline within the donjon?"
    A. It burned down.
    B. The narrator felt a sense of nervousness, horror, and fear.
    C. The men started to smell a strange, pungent stench coming from the room.
    D. Usher suddenly fell ill with the same symptoms she had had.

12. For what purpose does Poe include the details about the dark night and the unnatural light?
    A. He wants to mislead the reader so he/she won't suspect the ending.
    B. He wants to distract the reader from focusing on the death.
    C. He wants to add to the atmosphere of terror and suspense.
    D. He wants to impress the reader with his skills at writing details.

13. What happened as the narrator read the story to Roderick Usher?
    A. He heard cracking and ripping sounds, screaming and a metallic reverberation.
    B. He had heart palpations and was stricken momentarily blind.
    C. Usher suddenly began to cry.
    D. All of the lights in the house go out and the men are left in total darkness.

14. In the third paragraph from the end of this story, Poe uses repetition again to heighten the fantastic effect in the story. Which of these is <u>not</u> an example?
    A. Long-----long---long
    B. Many minutes, many hours, many days
    C. My dear, dear sister, my sister dear
    D. I dared not

15. What did the living corpse of Madeline do when it came into the narrator's room?
    A. It threw a dagger at Usher's heart.
    B. It began to shriek and wail.
    C. It disintegrated in front of their eyes.
    D. It fell on Usher.

16. What did the narrator do?
    A. He tried to pull the corpse off of Usher.
    B. He fled.
    C. He barricaded himself in his bedroom.
    D. He set the ghost on fire.

Fall of the House of Usher Multiple Choice Study Questions page 3

17. What happened to the House of Usher?
    A. It burned to the ground.
    B. It cracked and fell into pieces into the tarn.
    C. It exploded.
    D. The wind blew the roof off, and the inside was destroyed by water.

18. The *Fall of the House of Usher* is set in an old house. It is dark inside with tombs within. There is an eccentric hero and a living corpse. How is this type of story classified?
    A. It is science fiction.
    B. It is a medieval legend.
    C. It is a gothic story.
    D. It is a Renaissance adventure tale.

MULTIPLE CHOICE STUDY QUESTIONS - *The Murders in the Rue Morgue*

1. What is the purpose of Poe's discussing analytical power and ingenuity as well as chess and card games in the first four paragraphs of the story?
    - A. He wants to mislead the readers so the solution to the murders is not too obvious.
    - B. He sets out philosophy to prepare the reader for the methods of "the detective," Dupin.
    - C. He is trying to prove to his critics that he has a broad knowledge base and is qualified to be a writer of this of story.
    - D. He wants to be sure the reader has enough background to be able to understand the story.

2. Who is Dupin?
    - A. He is the detective.
    - B. H is the victim of the murder.
    - C. He is the Prefect of Police.
    - D. He is the sailor.

3. How did the narrator and Dupin meet?
    - A. They met at a rooming house where they were both staying.
    - B. They met at the library, where they were both looking for the same book.
    - C. They met on the train from Paris to Chantilly.
    - D. They met through a mutual friend who knew they both needed roommates.

4. How did they come to share the same flat?
    - A. The narrator was penniless and Dupin felt sorry for him.
    - B. Dupin offered to work for the narrator in return for lodging.
    - C. Dupin answered the narrator's ad in the paper for a roommate.
    - D. They decided to share expenses since they had common interests.

5. What was their daily life like at the flat?
    - A. They got up early, went for a long walk, read in the afternoon, and went to bed early in the evening. They didn't socialize much.
    - B. They usually slept all day and got up in time for dinner. Then they entertained or went out until early in the morning. After that they usually read or wrote for the rest of the night, and went to bed around sunrise.
    - C. They darkened the house during the day and stayed inside, reading and writing. Then they would go out for walks in the evening.
    - D. They entertained almost constantly, and always had a group of friends staying at the house. They played games, listened to music and danced. They did nothing intellectual.

6. Dupin says, "He is a very little fellow, that's true, and would do better for the Theatre des Varieties." What do we learn about Dupin from this statement and the explanation which follows?
    - A. We learn he does not like actors, because he thinks they don't do much.
    - B. We learn he is very critical and sarcastic.
    - C. We learn he is irrational, and quite subjective in his judgements. His only concern is making money.
    - D. We learn he has an acute eye for observing details and a logical analytical mind.

Murders in the Rue Morgue Multiple Choice Study Questions page 2

7. How did Dupin and the narrator first find out about the murders?
    A. The Prefect of Police told them.
    B. They lived in the same building and heard about it from the other tenants.
    C. They read about it in the newspaper.
    D. They were on their way to visit the murdered women, and discovered the bodies.

8. Many things were peculiar about the murders. Which of these was not mentioned in the story as being peculiar?
    A. There were fingerprints of three different people.
    B. The witnesses could not agree on the nationality of one of the voices they heard.
    C. There was no visible means of egress for the murderers.
    D. There were four thousand gold francs left in the room.

9. Why was Dupin so interested in the murders?
    A. He was sadistic by nature, and was fascinated by the gory details in the case.
    B. He had been romantically involved with Mademoiselle L'Espanaye and wanted to make sure whoever killed her was punished.
    C. He was looking for a way to get onto the police force. He thought solving the murders would show off his skills.
    D. He was intrigued because he was so naturally curious.

10. Why did Dupin become involved in the case?
    A. The family of the women offered him a large sum of money to investigate.
    B. The person accused of the murders had once helped him out, and he was grateful.
    C. He wanted to learn as much as he could, in order to write a book about the murders.
    D. He had a grudge against the Prefect of Police, and wanted to embarrass him by solving the murders first.

11. Three things confused the police. Which of these was not one of them?
    A. The time the murder was committed confused them.
    B. The absence of a means of escape confused them.
    C. The seeming impossibility of reconciling the voices they heard confused them.
    D. The absence of a motive confused them.

12. - 16. Dupin uncovered several facts that the police missed. Circle A if the sentence describes a fact Duping uncovered. Circle B if the sentence does not describe a fact uncovered by Dupin.

12. One window only appeared to be nailed shut, and was thus a means of entry and escape.
    A. Yes, Dupin uncovered this fact.
    B. No, Dupin did not uncover this fact.

13. The intruder climbed up the fire escape to get in.
    A. Yes, Dupin uncovered this fact.
    B. No, Dupin did not uncover this fact.

14. The marks on Mademoiselle L'Espanaye's neck matched those on an Ourang-Outang's hands.
    A. Yes, Dupin uncovered this fact.
    B. No, Dupin did not uncover this fact.

Murders in the Rue Morgue Multiple Choice Study Questions page 3

15. The hair Madame L'Espanaye clutched belonged to her daughter.
    A. Yes, Dupin uncovered this fact.
    B. No, Dupin did not uncover this fact.

16. There was a small piece of ribbon he thought to be from a sailor's hair, tied with a knot particular to the Maltese.
    A. Yes, Dupin uncovered this fact.
    B. No, Dupin did not uncover this fact.

17. How did Dupin test his theory and lure the suspect to his apartment?
    A. He let word out on the street through a series of informants.
    B. He had the narrator talk with the suspect. The narrator was blaming Dupin for the murders. Dupin thought this might get the suspect to talk, if he thought an innocent man might be convicted.
    C. He placed an ad in the paper looking for the owner of an ourang-outang.
    D. He put signs in the surrounding buildings offering a reward for any information about the murders.

18. What "reward" did Dupin want from the sailor?
    A. He wanted ten thousand dollars.
    B. He wanted the murderer to receive the death penalty.
    C. He wanted the sailor to let him (Dupin) bring the information to the Prefect of Police.
    D. He wanted all of the information about the murders.

19.-25. A series of events took place regarding the murders. Circle A if the sentence describes an event in the series. Circle B if the sentence does not describe an event in the series.

19. The sailor's Ourang-Outang watched him shave and escaped with a razor.
    A. Yes, this is one of the events that took place.
    B. No, this is not one of the events that took place.

20. He followed the women to their apartment and forced his way in.
    A. Yes, this is one of the events that took place.
    B. No, this is not one of the events that took place.

21. Madame L'Espanaye tried to take the razor away from him. He got angry and slit her throat.
    A. Yes, this is one of the events that took place.
    B. No, this is not one of the events that took place.

22. The blood frightened him; he grabbed the girl and strangled her in his frenzy.
    A. Yes, this is one of the events that took place.
    B. No, this is not one of the events that took place.

Murders in the Rue Morgue Multiple Choice Study Questions page 4

23. The Frenchman discovered what had happened and concealed the bodies.
    A. Yes, this is one of the events that took place.
    B. No, this is not one of the events that took place.

24. The Frenchman ran for home.
    A. Yes, this is one of the events that took place.
    B. No, this is not one of the events that took place.

25. The ourang-outang left through the window and closed the window behind itself.
    A. Yes, this is one of the events that took place.
    B. No, this is not one of the events that took place.

26. What was the reaction of the Prefect of Police to Dupin's solving the murders?
    A. He was neither happy or grateful. He told Dupin to mind his own business.
    B. He was so pleased that he offered Dupin a job.
    C. He refused to believe Dupin's solution and continued the investigation.
    D. He offered Dupin money if he would agree to say that the police had solved the murder.

27. Poe once again allows the reader to become more involved in the story. How does he do this?
    A. He uses several rhetorical questions that the reader can think about.
    B. He uses dashes instead of providing exact details so the reader can supply information.
    C. He makes extensive use of foreshadowing. If the reader is careful, he/she can follow Dupin's thinking and solve the mystery.
    D. He uses very specific names, dates, and locations to give the reader the sense of actually being there.

28. What is the narrator's function?
    A. He distracts us so that we can't solve the mystery.
    B. He gives us clues to help solve the mystery.
    C. He gives Dupin someone to interact with so that we can also see and understand the solution and how it came about.
    D. He provides a foil for Dupin. We are constantly reminded of Dupin's brilliance and the narrator's ineptness and stupidity.

29. At what point is the climax of the story?
    A. The climax occurs when the murder is committed.
    B. The climax occurs when Dupin takes his evidence to the police.
    C. The climax occurs when the bodies are discovered.
    D. The climax occurs when the sailor is confronted with providing an explanation for the murders.

MULTIPLE CHOICE STUDY QUESTIONS - *The Purloined Letter*

1. Who was Monsieur G--, and why had he come to see Dupin and the narrator?

    A. Monsieur G-- was the father of one of Dupin's old friends. He came to see if Dupin knew the whereabouts of his son, who seemed to have disappeared.
    B. He was a professor from the university. He wanted to offer a course in sleuthing, and came to Dupin for advice.
    C. He was the Prefect of Police. He came to see Dupin about a police matter.
    D. He was a local clergyman. He came to try and convince Dupin to join his church.

2. What is the problem G-- has come to discuss?
    A. A large sum of money has been stolen. Monsieur G-- suspects a friend of Dupin's, and wants his help to prove his theory.
    B. A letter has been stolen from the royal apartments. If the contents became known, it could cause damage to certain royalty.
    C. Monsieur G-- knows the contents of a letter that is in the possession of a rebel faction. If the military can get it, then they can beat the rebel forces. G-- wants Dupin to steal the letter.
    D. A collection of precious jewels, along with a detailed account of their history, has been stolen from the royal vault. G-- wants Dupin's help in finding the thief.

3. Who is D--?
    A. D-- is the narrator.
    B. D-- is the Prince.
    C. D-- is the Prefect's deputy.
    D. D-- is the thief.

4. Describe the police investigation of D--'s apartment.
    A. They searched every inch of it, and even used a microscope.
    B. They found the apartment in such a state of disarray that they just glanced over it. They didn't think they would be able to find anything.
    C. They were thorough, but they had forgotten to get a search warrant, so the evidence they found could not be used.
    D. The police were too busy to search thoroughly, so they only searched the living room.

5. When the Prefect returned a month later, what did Dupin give him?
    A. Dupin gave him a bill for his services.
    B. Dupin gave him the stolen letter.
    C. Dupin gave him two clues about the stolen letter
    D. Dupin gave him the name and location of the thief.

6. - 9. Dupin got the letter from D--. Some of the following statements describe his method. Fill in circle A if the sentence describes an event in the series. Circle B if the sentence does not describe an event in the series.

6. He went to visit D--, wearing dark glasses, so D-- couldn't see him looking around the room.
    A. Yes, this is one of the events that took place.
    B. No, this is not one of the events that took place.

Purloined Letter Multiple Choice Study Questions page 2

7. He found the letter and took it with him. He left his snuff box so he would have a reason to return to the apartment.
   A. Yes, this is one of the events that took place.
   B. No, this is not one of the events that took place.

8. He copied the letter at home and took the real one back to D--'s apartment the next day.
   A. Yes, this is one of the events that took place.
   B. No, this is not one of the events that took place.

9. He pre-arranged a diversion on the second day, and switched the letters, recovering the purloined letter.
   A. Yes, this is one of the events that took place.
   B. No, this is not one of the events that took place.

10. Why did Dupin replace the purloined letter with a facsimile?
    A. He did not want to be accused of the theft.
    B. He was hoping D-- would read the facsimile and get angry.
    C. He didn't want D-- to find the letter too soon, and he wanted to help cause D--'s political ruin.
    D. He was planning to blackmail D-- to get money for returning the real letter.

11. In "The Purloined Letter" the reader does not get to participate in the solving of the problem. We only get to read Dupin's account of how he solved it. Why? What is Poe trying to emphasize?
    A. He is trying to emphasize the use of logic and reasoning in solving a mystery.
    B. He is trying to show Dupin's superiority, both to the reader and to the other characters in the story.
    C. He is trying to keep the reader more involved by forcing him/her to anticipate future events.
    D. He is trying to emphasize that he, as a writer, has complete control of the story.

12. Again, as in many of his stories, Poe emphasizes the method of solution. How does he do this?
    A. He keeps the story at a certain length.
    B. He omits details such as people's names.
    C. He makes frequent use of figurative language.
    D. He plants subtle clues that a careful reader can discover.

13. G-- says, "but then he is a poet, which I take to be only one removed from a fool." What does Dupin say this reasoning by G-- caused?
    A. G--'s obvious prejudice cost him the good will of his men, and he lost their cooperation.
    B. G--'s statement cost him a promotion, because his immediate superior was an amateur poet.
    C. This statement caused a lot of friction and hostility between the police department and the city's literary circles.
    D. It caused G-- to underestimate D--'s abilities in using logic and reason.

Purloined Letter Multiple Choice Study Questions page 3

14. "Perhaps it is the very simplicity of the thing which puts you at fault." What does Dupin mean?
    A. G-- thought of himself as so brilliant that he kept himself from solving the case.
    B. The detectives are trained to do much harder work. They thought this case was going to be easy, so they were careless. This caused them to make mistakes.
    C. The detectives were so busy looking for a small clue that they missed the obvious clues. Dupin thought about the person and his motives to help him find the letter.
    D. Hard work is often more beneficial than brilliant thinking.

15. "...occasions may occur when x^2+px is not altogether equal to q..." Explain.
    A. Dupin found that a solid foundation in mathematics helped him to find clues that he otherwise might have missed.
    B. Things aren't always as they appear. One needs to keep an open mind.
    C. Dupin was referring to G--. He meant that some people look capable, but really are not.
    D. A mistake in calculations is just as damaging for a detective as it is for a mathematician.

MULTIPLE CHOICE STUDY QUESTIONS - *The Pit and the Pendulum*

1. What is the first scene the narrator describes?
    A. He describes his arrest, when he was dragged from his home.
    B. He describes the courtroom scene when he was sentenced to death.
    C. He describes his first day of torture.
    D. He describes being rescued.

2. After "swooning" and describing various states of being conscious, where does the narrator come to his senses?
    A. He is in a small bedroom in a monastery.
    B. He is in the courtroom.
    C. He is in his own living room.
    D. He is in a pitch-dark dungeon.

3. How did the narrator first explore his surroundings?
    A. He rolled across the floor and counted the number of seconds it took.
    B. He walked against the wall in a straight line and counted his footsteps, so that he could pace off the size of the room.
    C. He placed a piece of cloth at a right angle from the wall on the floor to mark his beginning point and followed the wall.
    D. He crawled on his hands and knees along one wall, but then he got scared and stopped.

4. In what way did he venture to explore after his first circuit? What problem did he encounter?
    A. He crossed the room in a direct line. He fell on his face and discovered the pit.
    B. He crossed the room diagonally and discovered the pendulum.
    C. He crossed the room in a direct line and discovered that the floor was covered with nails and broken glass.
    D. He tried climbing one of the walls, but it was too slippery from moss and dampness.

5. After they realized he would now cautiously avoid the pit, what fate did the narrator's captors plan for him?
    A. They tied him to the ground, spread honey on him, and released a colony of ants and a hive of bees.
    B. They used two thin ropes to hang him over a large vat of boiling oil. The more he moved, the faster the ropes lost their strength, and he would fall into the oil.
    C. They brought in his family and told him he would have to watch them be killed before he died.
    D. They tied him to a table over which a razor sharp, steel crescent slowly descended. They intended for him to be repeatedly sliced and for him to bleed to death.

6. What else was in the room with the narrator?
    A. There were three other persons.
    B. There were snakes.
    C. There were rats.
    D. There were two priests urging him to confess.

Pit and the Pendulum Multiple Choice Study Questions page 2

7. How did the narrator get free from the table under the pendulum?
    A. He pulled at the ropes and stretched them until they were loose enough for him to move out of the way.
    B. He wiped his food over the parts of the ropes he could reach so the rats would eat through them.
    C. He rocked from side to side until he manage to tilt the table on its side. Then the pendulum cut through the ropes and he rolled out of the way.
    D. He pretended to be dead and the captors stopped the pendulum, retracted it, and untied him. When they saw that he was alive they thought of another torture.

8. After the narrator became free from the table, he was subjected to yet another means toward death. What was it?
    A. The room was slowly being filled with water, which would eventually drown him.
    B. The walls of the room began to move inward, pushing him toward to the pit.
    C. Poisonous snakes and insects were dropped into the room from above.
    D. The only air vent was covered, so that he would suffocate.

9. Just as he was about to be forced into the pit, what happened?
    A. He had a heart attack.
    B. His family arrived with enough money to buy his freedom.
    C. He was saved; the Inquisition was over.
    D. He woke up and realized he had been hallucinating due to a high fever.

10. One of Poe's trademarks is that he uses all of his literary tools to produce a single effect for the reader. What is the effect given by this story?
    A. It is disgust that man could behave so terribly in the name of religion.
    B. The effect is astonishment at the surprise ending.
    C. It is a feeling of an individual's powerlessness over his fate.
    D. The effect is the feeling of terror--the fear of inevitable death.

11. What effect does the ending (the narrator's being saved) have on us as readers?
    A. It is one of belief in the ultimate goodness of mankind.
    B. It is one of surprise and relief.
    C. It is one of thankfulness at not being alive during the time of the Inquisition.
    D. It is one of disbelief that such a story could have a happy ending.

12. One of Poe's favorite conflicts is that of madness vs. reason. How is that conflict resolved in this story?
    A. Reason wins.
    B. Conflict wins.
    C. Reason and conflict balance each other equally.
    D. Poe never settles the conflict.

13. There are many references to "hope" in this story. According to Poe, is there hope?
    A. No. Some situations are hopeless.
    B. Yes, there is always hope.

Pit and the Pendulum Multiple Choice Study Questions page 3

14. Where is the climax of the story?
    A. The climax is when he frees himself from the ropes.
    B. The climax is at the very end as he is about to finally be pushed into the pit.
    C. The climax is when he first discovers the pit.
    D. The climax is when he is rescued.

15. The story has a dark chamber (dungeon) presumably in some larger castle-like building, grotesque torture, struggle between life/consciousness and death/unconsciousness, and a feeling of terror and fear. What genre does this describe?
    A. It describes science fiction.
    B. It describes historical fiction.
    C. It describes existentialism.
    D. It describes a gothic tale.

MULTIPLE CHOICE STUDY QUESTIONS - *The Masque of Red Death*

1. What was the Red Death?
    A. It was an algae contamination that turned all of the water red. Anyone who drank the water died.
    B. It was a series of brutal, bloody murders. The murders always left a red handkerchief at the scene of the crime.
    C. It was a highly contagious disease.
    D. It was a red rope that the at the prince always used to hang his enemies.

2. Why did Prince Prospero gather 1,000 of his subjects into his castle?
    A. He wanted them to witness the baptism of his youngest son.
    B. He wanted to save those in his kingdom who had not yet died from the Red Death.
    C. He knew the peasants were planning a revolt. He wanted to have as many of his followers as possible near him for protection.
    D. He needed money. He was holding them captive until their family members paid large ransoms.

3. How many rooms were in use the night of the masquerade ball?
    A. Eighteen rooms were in use.
    B. Thirty rooms were in use.
    C. One hundred twenty rooms were in use.
    D. Seven rooms were in use.

4. In most of the rooms, the stained glass windows were of the same color as the rest of the decorations. In which room were the windows a different color?
    A. They were different in the red room.
    B. They were different in the black room.
    C. They were different in the purple room.
    D. They were different in the white room.

5. For what did the orchestra pause each hour?
    A. They paused for the striking of the ebony clock.
    B. They paused for the blessing of the hour by the priest.
    C. They paused for refreshments.
    D. They paused to let the Prince play a tune on the piano.

6. Why did the newly masqued figure draw attention?
    A. It had only a right arm and a left leg.
    B. It had real blood flowing from several wounds.
    C. It was dressed as a corpse of someone who had died of the Read Death.
    D. It arrived in a fine coach with several servants. It refused to speak to anyone.

7. What was Prince Prosper's reaction to the figure?
    A. He bellowed that someone should unmask the figure.
    B. He treated the figure like royalty.
    C. He ordered his guards to kill the figure.
    D. He urged the other guests to ignore the uninvited intruder.

8. What did the other guests realize when they went into the black room?
    A. The figure was really the Princess, playing a trick on them.
    B. They were locked in and could not escape--the Price had tricked them!
    C. They could see that it was morning, and they were safe.
    D. They discovered that no tangible form inhabited the costume.

Masque of Red Death Multiple Choice Study Questions page 2

9. How did the story end?
    A. The Prince killed everyone in his rage at the intruder.
    B. Everyone in the room contracted the disease and died.
    C. The people all panicked. In their panic, they killed one another.
    D. The Prince died, but the others survived.

10. What is the moral of the story?
    A. Royalty in itself is not a protection.
    B. You can't hide from death.
    C. Debauchery in the face of illness will be punished.
    D. All men are sinners.

11. What single effect was Poe trying to convey?
    A. He was conveying despair.
    B. He was conveying greed.
    C. He was conveying horror.
    D. He was conveying hatred.

12. There are many gothic influences in The Masque of the Red Death. Which of these is not a gothic influence?
    A. A castle is not a gothic influence.
    B. The long ago/far away setting is not a gothic influence.
    C. The crossing over of life to death is not a gothic influence.
    D. The use of many different colors is not a gothic influence.

13. Where is the climax of the story?
    A. The climax is when the people realize the Red Death has come.
    B. The climax is when the others first see the corpse-like figure.
    C. The climax is when the last of the guests dies.
    D. The climax is when the Prince first sees the figure.

14. The Prince's name is a play on the word "prosperous." He is in reality a prince without prosperity, without life or a kingdom at the end of the party. What figure of speech does Poe use here?
    A. He uses onomatopoeia.
    B. He use satire.
    C. He uses irony.
    D. He uses melodrama.

15. Explain the significance of "three thousand and six hundred seconds to the Time that flies."
    A. Some people, like the prince, are very interested in details.
    B. Life's fleeting moments often slip by.
    C. Death is a natural part of life.
    D. Machines go on even when human life ends.

MULTIPLE CHOICE STUDY QUESTIONS - *The Cask of Amontillado*

1. Why did Montresor decide to kill Fortunato?
    A. Montresor decided to kill Fortunato because Fortunato had stolen a large sum of money from him and refused to repay it.
    B. Montresor decided to kill Fortunato because Fortunato wanted to marry his sister. Montresor was very jealous and possessive, and didn't want his sister to marry anyone.
    C. Montresor decided to kill Fortunato because Fortunato had insulted him.
    D. Montresor decided to kill Fortunato because he simple wanted to have the experience of killing someone.

2. Fortunato's name implies that he is fortunate, although he is really not. What literary form is this?
    A. This is alliteration.
    B. This is irony.
    C. This is foreshadowing.
    D. This is exaggeration.

3. What was Fortunato's weak point, and how did Montresor capitalize on it?
    A. Fortunato loved going to the theater, so Montresor invited him to a play, knowing they would be out late.
    B. Fortunato loved wines and considered himself a connoisseur.
    C. Fortunato loved money. Montresor offered to pay him to help repair the wine cellar, and Fortunato agreed.
    D. Fortunato loved dancing. Montresor told him he was having a party the next week, and asked Fortunato to teach him some dance steps.

4. How does Montresor insure Fortunato will come along?
    A. He cries and begs, because he knows Fortunato has a soft heart.
    B. He also invites a woman in whom Fortunato is interested.
    C. He offers to pay Fortunato a large sum of money.
    D. He insinuates that Luchesi can complete the task if Fortunato is busy. He knows Fortunato won't miss a chance to prove his capabilities.

5. Why does Fortunato continue underground among the catacombs when the nitre is making his cough worse?
    A. He is too proud to turn back and let someone else finish the task.
    B. He is too drunk to notice that he is coughing.
    C. He loves Montresor, and doesn't want to disappoint him.
    D. He is secretly afraid of the dark, and doesn't want to go back alone.

6. As they continue, what does Montresor offer to Fortunato? Why?
    A. He offers him an extra candle to ally his fears.
    B. He offers him a blanket to keep warm. He doesn't want Fortunato to give up.
    C. He offers him wine to defend him from the dampness. He is actually getting Fortunato drunk.
    D. He offers him half of the wine in his cellar. He does this to prove to himself that Fortunato is greedy.

Cask of Amontillado Multiple Choice Study Questions page 2

7. What "sign" of the masons did Montresor give Fortunato?
    A. He showed a trowel.
    B. He showed a bag of cement.
    C. He showed a hammer.
    D. He showed a chisel.

8. What did Montresor do to Fortunato when they reached the recess where the Amontillado was supposed to be?
    A. Montresor hit Fortunato over the head with a bottle of the wine and then tied him to a chair.
    B. Montresor tripped Fortunato and chained him to the floor when he fell.
    C. Montresor stabbed Fortunato several times and locked him in a vault.
    D. Montresor followed Fortunato and chained him to a granite wall.

9. Why didn't Fortunato resist?
    A. He was too frightened.
    B. He was dumbfounded and drunk.
    C. He thought Montresor was just joking.
    D. He thought if he didn't resist at first, he could catch Montresor by surprise later.

10. How did Montresor kill Fortunato?
    A. He forced him to drink poisoned wine.
    B. He beat him to death with some stays from one of the oak wine barrels.
    C. He bricked up the recess so there was no hope of escape.
    D. He stabbed him through the heart.

11. Why did Montresor's "heart grow sick?"
    A. He regretted what he had done to Fortunato.
    B. He realized he could never come into his wine cellar again, and he knew he would miss having the wine.
    C. He didn't like the dampness in the catacombs.
    D. He suddenly became overpowered by the nitre and had a heart attack.

12. In the last portion of the story, Montresor often repeats Fortunato's words. What effect does this have?
    A. It shows his cold-heartedness, perhaps his madness.
    B. It focuses the reader's attention on the climax of the story.
    C. It gives the reader a felling of pity for both of the characters.
    D. It shows Fortunato's increasing sobriety.

13. What is ironic about the trowel?
    A. Fortunato had given it to Montresor several years before as a gift, and now Montresor was using it to kill him.
    B. It is such a small tool to do such a large and horrible job.
    C. It was the tool of entombment, but it could also have been the tool of escape.
    D. It is a sign of the Mason and Montresor used it just after Fortunato claimed Montresor was not good enough to be a Mason.

Cask of Amontillado Multiple Choice Study Questions page 3

14. Montresor shows one ordinary, friendly side to Fortunato. But, he has another side which is mad/irrational toward the end of the story. What does this show?
    A. It shows Poe's skill at character development.
    B. It shows things are not always as they seem.
    C. It shows Montresor's double personality.
    D. It shows how one person (Fortunato) can bring out the worst in another (Montresor).

15. What is ironic about the time of the murder?
    A. It happened on the anniversary of the day Montresor and Fortunato first met each other.
    B. It is carnival time, a happy time.
    C. It is Lent, a holy season when people atone for their sins.
    D. It is Fortunato's birthday.

16. There are may gothic elements present in this story. Which of these is not a gothic element?
    A. The use of catacombs is not a gothic element.
    B. The use of a large, old mansion is not a gothic element.
    C. The use of wine and other alcoholic beverages is not a gothic element.
    D. The contrast between life and death is not a gothic element.

17. What does the first person narrative technique add to this story?
    A. It helps get the reader involved and it helps creates suspense.
    B. It is a change from Poe's usual third person narrative, so readers who have read many of his stories will be introduced to a new approach, and won't get bored with his style.
    C. It keeps us focused on the narrator instead of on the unfortunate victim.
    D. It is easier to follow the main character's motive.

ANSWER KEY - MULTIPLE CHOICE STUDY/QUIZ QUESTIONS
E. A. Poe Stories

The Tell-Tale Heart

1. A	11. A
2. C	12. C
3. D	13. C
4. B	14. B
5. C	15. A
6. A	16. D
7. C	17. B
8. D	18. A
9. B	19. C
10. D	20. B

The Black Cat

1. C	10. B
2. A	11. C
3. D	12. C
4. B	13. D
5. B	14. B
6. C	15. C
7. D	16. A
8. A	17. D
9. D	18. A

House of Usher

1. D	10. A
2. B	11. B
3. C	12. C
4. A	13. A
5. B	14. C
6. D	15. D
7. C	16. B
8. C	17. B
9. D	18. C

The Murders in the Rue Morgue

1. B	16. A
2. A	17. C
3. B	18. D
4. D	19. A
5. C	20. B
6. D	21. B
7. C	22. A
8. A	23. B
9. D	24. A
10. B	25. A
11. A	26. A
12. A	27. B
13. B	28. C
14. A	29. D
15. B	

The Purloined Letter

1. C	11. A
2. B	12. B
3. D	13. D
4. A	14. C
5. B	15. B
6. A	
7. B	
8. B	
9. A	
10. C	

The Pit and the Pendulum

1. B	11. B
2. D	12. A
3. C	13. B
4. A	14. B
5. D	15. D
6. C	
7. B	
8. B	
9. C	
10. D	

The Masque of the Red Death

1. C	11. C
2. B	12. D
3. D	13. A
4. B	14. C
5. A	15. B
6. C	
7. A	
8. D	
9. B	
10. B	

The Cask of Amontillado

1. C	10. C
2. B	11. C
3. B	12. A
4. D	13. D
5. A	14. C
6. C	15. B
7. A	16. C
8. D	17. A
9. B	

PREREADING VOCABULARY WORKSHEETS

VOCABULARY - *Poe Stories*

Vocabulary - *The Tell-Tale Heart*
Part I: Using Prior Knowledge and Contextual Clues
   Below are the sentences in which the vocabulary words appear in the text. Read the sentence. Use any clues you can find in the sentence combined with your prior knowledge, and write what you think the underlined words mean on the lines provided.

1. It is impossible to say how first the idea entered my brain; but once conceived, it haunted me day and night.

2. You should have seen how wisely I proceeded with what caution--with what foresight--with what dissimulation I went to work!

3. ...it was not the old man who vexed me, but his Evil Eye.

4. ...I felt the extent of my own powers--of my sagacity.

5. He was still sitting up in the bed listening;--just as I have done, night after night, hearkening to the death watches in the wall.

6. And it was the mournful influence of the unperceived shadow that caused him to feel...the presence of my head within the room.

7. And now have I not told you that what you mistake for madness is but over-acuteness of the senses?

8. ...I myself, in the wild audacity of my perfect triumph, I placed my own seat upon the very spot beneath which reposed the corpse of the victim.

9. ...they were making a mockery of my horror!...Anything was more tolerable than this derision!

Part II: Determining the Meaning -- Match the vocabulary words to their definitions.
___ 1. conceived
___ 2. dissimulation
___ 3. vexed
___ 4. sagacity
___ 5. hearkening
___ 6. unperceived
___ 7. acuteness
___ 8. audacity
___ 9. derision

A. The quality of being discerning, sound in judgment
B. Boldness; daring
C. Scoffing; ridicule
D. To form or develop in the mind; devise
E. Reacting readily to impressions; sensitive
F. Concealing one's true feelings or intentions
G. To bring distress or suffering to; plague or afflict
H. Unnoticed
I. Listening

Vocabulary - *The Cask of Amontillado*

Part I: Using Prior Knowledge and Contextual Clues

Below are the sentences in which the vocabulary words appear in the text. Read the sentence. Use any clues you can find in the sentence combined with your prior knowledge, and write what you think the underlined words mean on the lines provided.

1. The thousand <u>injuries</u> of Fortunato I had borne as I best could; but when he ventured upon insult, I vowed revenge.

2. I must not only punish, but punish with <u>impunity</u>.

3. ...that my smile now was at the thought of his <u>immolation</u>.

4. You have been <u>imposed</u> upon.

5. We came at length to the foot of the descent, and stood together on the damp ground of the <u>catacombs</u>....

6. ...looked into my eyes with two filmy <u>orbs</u> that distilled the rheum of intoxication.

7. "You are not of the <u>masons</u>."

8. ...the foulness of the air caused our <u>flambeaux</u> rather to glow than flame.

9. ...bones had been thrown down, and lay <u>promiscuously</u> upon the earth.

Part II. Determining the Meaning -- Match the vocabulary words to their definitions.

___ 1. injuries
___ 2. impunity
___ 3. immolation
___ 4. imposed
___ 5. catacombs
___ 6. orbs
___ 7. masons
___ 8. flambeaux
___ 9. promiscuously

A. Casually; randomly
B. One who builds or works with stone or brick
C. Forced on another or others
D. Damage or harm done to or suffered by a person or thing
E. Underground cemetery
F. Exemption from punishment, penalty, or harm
G. Eyes
H. Destruction; being killed
I. A lighted torch

Vocabulary - *The Black Cat*

Part I: Using Prior Knowledge and Contextual Clues
Read the sentence. Use any clues you can find in the sentence combined with your prior knowledge, and write what you think the underlined words mean on the lines provided.

1. I suffered myself to use <u>intemperate</u> language to my wife.

2. My original soul seemed, at once, to take its flight from my body; and a more than fiendish <u>malevolence</u>, gin-nurtured, thrilled every fibre of my frame.

3-4. And then came, as if to my final and <u>irrevocable</u> overthrow, the spirit of <u>perverseness</u>.

5. I am above the weakness of seeking to establish a sequence of cause and effect, between the disaster and the <u>atrocity</u>.

6. When I first beheld this <u>apparition</u>--for I could scarcely regard it as less--my wonder and my terror were extreme.

7. ...I came to look upon it with unutterable loathing, and to flee silently from its <u>odious</u> presence, as from the breath of a pestilence.

8. It followed my footsteps with a <u>pertinacity</u> which would be difficult to make the reader comprehend.

9. ...the feeble remnant of the good within me <u>succumbed</u>. Evil thoughts became my sole intimates...

10. Upon its head,...sat the hideous beast whose craft had...whose voice had <u>consigned</u> me to the hangman.

Part II. Determining the Meaning -- Match the vocabulary words to their definitions

___ 1. intemperate   A. Can't be turned back
___ 2. malevolence   B. Quality of being directed away from what is
___ 3. irrevocable   right or good
___ 4. perverseness   C. Not moderate
___ 5. atrocity   D. A ghostly figure
___ 6. apparition   E. Handed over
___ 7. odious   F. Ill will toward others; rancor; malice; evil
___ 8. pertinacity   influence, especially supernatural
___ 9. succumbed   G. An appalling or atrocious action, situation, or object
___ 10. consigned   H. Gave in
                      I. Evoking feelings or repulsion
                      J. Persistence; tenacity; without quitting

Vocabulary - *The Masque Of The Red Death*

Part I: Using Prior Knowledge and Contextual Clues

Below are the sentences in which the vocabulary words appear in the text. Read the sentence. Use any clues you can find in the sentence combined with your prior knowledge, and write what you think the underlined words mean on the lines provided.

1. No <u>pestilence</u> had ever been so fatal, or so hideous.

_____

2. This was an extensive and magnificent structure, the creation of the prince's own eccentric yet <u>august</u> taste.

_____

3. It was a <u>voluptuous</u> scene, the masquerade.

_____

4. ... the view of the whole extent is scarcely <u>impeded</u>.

_____

5. ...produced so wild a look upon the <u>countenances</u>.

_____

6. ...it was a gay and magnificent <u>revel.</u>

_____

7. He had directed, in great part, the movable <u>embellishments</u> of the seven chambers.

_____

8. ...there comes from the near clock of ebony a muffled peal more solemnly <u>emphatic</u> than any which reaches their ears who indulge in the more remote gaieties of the other apartments.

_____

9. In truth the <u>masquerade</u> license of the night was nearly unlimited...

_____

Part II. Determining the Meaning -- Match the vocabulary words to their definitions.

___ 1. pestilence
___ 2. august
___ 3. voluptuous
___ 4. impeded
___ 5. countenances
___ 6. revel
___ 7. embellishments
___ 8. emphatic
___ 9. masquerade

A. Giving, unrestrained pleasure to the senses
B. Ornaments
C. A usually fatal epidemic disease
D. A costume party; disguise or false outward show
E. Inspiring awe or admiration; majestic
F. Obstructed
G. Festivity or celebration
H. Faces
I. Bold and definite in expression or action

Vocabulary - *The Fall of the House of Usher*

Part I: Using Prior Knowledge and Contextual Clues

Below are the sentences in which the vocabulary words appear in the text. Read the sentence. Use any clues you can find in the sentence combined with your prior knowledge, and write what you think the underlined words mean on the lines provided.

1. ...a mere different arrangement of the particulars of the scene...helps to <u>annihilate</u> its capacity for sorrowful. impression...

2. ...I really knew little of my friend. His <u>reserve</u> had been always excessive and habitual.

3. Perhaps the eye of a scrutinizing observer might have discovered a barely perceptible <u>fissure</u>, which...made its way down the wall in a zigzag direction...

4. ...I soon found this to arise from a series of feeble and futile struggles to overcome an habitual <u>trepidance</u>--an excessive nervous agitation.

5. To an <u>anomalous</u> species of terror I found him a bounden slave.

6. His long improvised <u>dirges</u> will ring forever in my ears.

7. One of the <u>phantasmagoric</u> conceptions of my friend,...may be shadowed forth, although feebly, in words.

8. An irrepressible tremor gradually pervaded my frame; and at length, there sat upon my very heart an <u>incubus</u> of utterly causeless alarm.

9. ...there is little in its uncouth and unimaginative <u>prolixity</u> which could have had interest for the lofty and spiritual ideality of my friend.

10. ... my brain reeled as I saw the mighty walls rushing <u>asunder</u>.

Fall of the House of Usher Vocabulary Part II

Part II: Determining the Meaning -- Match the vocabulary words to their definitions.

    ____ 1. annihilate
    ____ 2. reserve
    ____ 3. fissure
    ____ 4. trepidance
    ____ 5. anomalous
    ____ 6. dirges
    ____ 7. phantasmagoric
    ____ 8. incubus
    ____ 9. prolixity
    ____ 10. asunder

A. A fantastic sequence of haphazardly associated imagery
B. Into separate parts or pieces
C. Slow, mournful music compositions
D. To reduce to nonexistence; to nullify or render void; abolish
E. Wordiness
F. Abnormal
G. An oppressive or nightmarish burden
H. The keeping of one's feelings, thought, or affairs to oneself
I. A state of alarm or dread; apprehension; involuntary trembling or quivering
J. A crack

Vocabulary - *The Murders in the Rue Morgue*

Part I: Using Prior Knowledge and Contextual Clues

Below are the sentences in which the vocabulary words appear in the text. Read the sentence. Use any clues you can find in the sentence combined with your prior knowledge, and write what you think the underlined words mean on the lines provided.

1. The higher powers of the reflective intellect are more decidedly and more usefully tasked by the unostentatious game of draughts than by all the elaborate frivolity of chess.

2. These are not only manifold, but multiform...

3. But it is in matters beyond the limits of mere rule that the skill of the analyst is evinced.

4. ...by a variety of untoward events, [he] had been reduced to such poverty that the energy of his character succumbed beneath it, and he ceased to bestir himself in the world...

5. ...there still remained in his possession a small remnant of his patrimony...

6. It was a freak of fancy in my friend...to be enamored of the night...

7. Here I paused, to ascertain beyond a doubt whether he really knew of whom I thought.

8. You stepped upon one of the loose fragments, slipped, slightly strained your ankle appeared vexed or sulky, muttered a few words, turned to look at the pile, and then proceeded in silence.

9. You thought of the poor cobbler's immolation.

10. Upon examining it, my excoriations were perceived.

Part II. Determining the Meaning -- Match the vocabulary words to their definitions.

___ 1. unostentatious   A. Scrapes
___ 2. manifold   B. Showed or demonstrated clearly
___ 3. evinced   C. Gave in
___ 4. succumbed   D. Unpretentious; not showy
___ 5. patrimony   E. Inheritance
___ 6. enamored   F. One of many kinds
___ 7. ascertained   G. To find out
___ 8. vexed   H. Inspired; captivated
___ 9. immolation   I. Bothered
___ 10. excoriations   J. Death; destruction

The Murders in the Rue Morgue - Vocabulary Worksheet Page 2

11. <u>Corroborates</u> the general testimony.

12. The corpse of the young lady was much bruised and <u>excoriated</u>.

13. There were several deep scratches just below the chin, together with a series of <u>livid</u> spots which were evidently the impression of fingers.

14. A heavy club of wood, or a broad bar of iron--a chair--any large, heavy, and <u>obtuse</u> weapon would have produced such results...

15. ...but not being <u>cognizant</u> of that tongue, is like the Spaniard, `convinced by the intonation.'

16. the means of <u>egress</u> employed by the murderers.

17. This...has been justly characterized by one of the witness...as expression of remonstrance or <u>expostulation</u>...

18. You have done nothing which you could have avoided--nothing, certainly, which renders you <u>culpable</u>.

19. You were not even guilty of robbery, when you might have robbed with <u>impunity</u>.

Part II: Determining the Meaning -- Match the vocabulary words to their definitions.

___ 11. corroborates
___ 12. excoriated
___ 13. livid
___ 14. obtuse
___ 15. cognizant
___ 16. egress
___ 17. expostulation
___ 18. culpable
___ 19. impunity

A. Scraped
B. Reasoning earnestly with someone in an effort to dissuade or correct
C. To strengthen or support with other evidence
D. Bruised
E. Blunt
F. Without punishment
G. Aware of; familiar with
H. Exit; escape
I. Responsible; at fault

Vocabulary - *The Purloined Letter*

Part I: Using Prior Knowledge and Contextual Clues

Below are the sentences in which the vocabulary words appear in the text. Read the sentence. Use any clues you can find in the sentence combined with your prior knowledge, and write what you think the underlined words mean on the lines provided.

1. ...certain document of the last importance has been <u>purloined</u> from the royal apartments.

_____

2. ..."no more <u>sagacious</u> agent could, I suppose, be desired, or even imagined."

_____

3. ...I did not abandon the search until I had become fully satisfied that the thief is a more <u>astute</u> man than myself.

_____

4. "We had; but the reward offered is <u>prodigious</u>."

_____

5. The mathematicians, I grant you, have done their best to <u>promulgate</u> the popular error to which you allude...

_____

6. And this error is so <u>egregious</u> that I am confounded at the universality with which it has been received.

_____

7. ...these things, I say, were strongly <u>corroborative</u> of suspicion, in one who came with the intention to suspect.

_____

8. His downfall, too, will not be more <u>precipitate</u> than awkward.

_____

Part II: Determining the Meaning -- Match the vocabulary words to their definitions.

___ 1. purloined
___ 2. sagacious
___ 3. astute
___ 4. prodigious
___ 5. promulgate
___ 6. egregious
___ 7. corroborative
___ 8. precipitate

A. Moving rapidly and heedlessly
B. Reenforcing
C. Bad or offensive
D. To make known
E. Enormous
F. Shrewd
G. Wise
H. Stolen

Vocabulary - *The Pit And The Pendulum*

Part I: Using Prior Knowledge and Contextual Clues

Below are the sentences in which the vocabulary words appear in the text. Read the sentence. Use any clues you can find in the sentence combined with your prior knowledge, and write what you think the underlined words mean on the lines provided.

1. I saw them writhe with a deadly <u>locution</u>.

___

2-3. ...I have conjured up remembrances which the <u>lucid</u> reason of a later <u>epoch</u> assures me could have had reference only to that condition of seeming unconsciousness.

___

4. This process, however, afforded me no means of <u>ascertaining</u> the dimensions of my dungeon...

___

5-6. My <u>cognizance</u> of the pit had become known to the inquisitorial agents--the pit whose horrors had been destined for so bold a <u>recusant</u> as myself...

___

7. ...I felt very--oh! inexpressibly--sick and weak, as if through long <u>inanition</u>.

___

8. In their <u>voracity</u>, the vermin frequently fastened their sharp fangs in my fingers.

___

Part II: Determining the Meaning -- Match the vocabulary words to their definitions.

___ 1. locution   A. Wild hunger
___ 2. lucid   B. Easily understood; sane or rational
___ 3. epoch   C. Exhaustion, as of from lack of nourishment
___ 4. ascertaining   D. Awareness
___ 5. cognizance   E. Style of speaking
___ 6. recusant   F. Age; time
___ 7. inanition   G. A non-conformist
___ 8. voracity   H. Finding out

Vocabulary - *The Raven*

Part I: Using Prior Knowledge and Contextual Clues

Below are the sentences in which the vocabulary words appear in the text. Read the sentence. Use any clues you can find in the sentence combined with your prior knowledge, and write what you think the underlined words mean on the lines provided.

1. And each separate dying ember <u>wrought</u> its ghost upon the floor.

_____

2. Not the least <u>obeisance</u> made he; not a minute stopped or stayed he,...

_____

3. But, with <u>mien</u> of lord or lady, perched above my chamber door---

_____

4. Then this ebony bird <u>beguiling</u> my sad fancy into smiling,...

_____

5. the <u>dirges</u> of his Hope that melancholy burden bore...

_____

6. ...thinking what this <u>ominous</u> bird of your--.../ Meant in croaking "Nevermore."

_____

7. And the Raven, never flitting, still is sitting, still is sitting/On the <u>pallid</u> bust of Pallas...

_____

Part II: Determining the Meaning -- Match the vocabulary words to their definitions.

___ 1. wroughtA. Funeral hymns or lamentations; slow, mournful music
___ 2. obeisance
___ 3. mienB. Menacing; threatening
___ 4. beguilingC. Deceiving; diverting
___ 5. dirgesD. Pale, dull
___ 6. ominousE. Movement of the body that expresses deference or homage
___ 7. pallid
F. Manner
G. Created

Vocabulary - *Lenore*

Part I: Using Prior Knowledge and Contextual Clues

Below are the sentences in which the vocabulary words appear in the text. Read the sentence. Use any clues you can find in the sentence combined with your prior knowledge, and write what you think the underlined words mean on the lines provided.

1-2. See on yon drear and rigid <u>bier</u> low lies thy love, Lenore!/come! let the burial rite be read-- the funeral song be sung!--/An <u>anthem</u> for the queenliest dead that ever died so young.

_____

_____

3. ...the <u>requiem</u> how be sung...

_____

4-5. But waft the angel on her flight with <u>paean</u> of old days!/Let no bell toll!--lest her sweet soul, amid its <u>hallowed</u> mirth,/Should catch the note,

_____

_____

Part II: Determining the Meaning -- Match the vocabulary words to their definitions.

___ 1. bier
___ 2. anthem
___ 3. requiem
___ 4. paean
___ 5. hallowed

A. Holy; reverent
B. Stand on which a corpse or a coffin is placed before burial
C. Song of joyful praise
D. A hymn of praise or loyalty
E. A hymn, composition, or service for the dead

Vocabulary - *To Helen*

Part I: Using Prior Knowledge and Contextual Clues

Below are the sentences in which the vocabulary words appear in the text. Read the sentence. Use any clues you can find in the sentence combined with your prior knowledge, and write what you think the underlined words mean on the lines provided.

1. A full-orbed moon,...Sought a precipitate pathway up through heaven,

_____

2. With quietude, and sultriness, and slumber,

_____

3-4. Their odorous souls in ecstatic death--

_____

_____

5. How dark a woe! yet how sublime a hope!

_____

6. How fathomless a capacity for love!

_____

7. And thou, a ghost amid the entombing trees

_____

8. While even in the meridian glare of day/I see them still

_____

Part II: Determining the Meaning -- Match the vocabulary words to their definitions.

___ 1. precipitate
___ 2. sultriness
___ 3. odorous
___ 4. ecstatic
___ 5. sublime
___ 6. fathomless
___ 7. amid
___ 8. meridian

A. Marked by excessive haste
B. Having a distinct odor
C. Too deep to be measured
D. Euphoric; blissful
E. The highest point in the sky reached by the sun
F. In the middle of
G. Majestic; inspiring awe; impressive
H. Sensualness; voluptuousness

Vocabulary - *Ulalume*

Part I: Using Prior Knowledge and Contextual Clues

Below are the sentences in which the vocabulary words appear in the text. Read the sentence. Use any clues you can find in the sentence combined with your prior knowledge, and write what you think the underlined words mean on the lines provided.

1. These were days when my heart was volcanic/As the scoria rivers that roll--

2. In the realms of the boreal pole.

3. But our thoughts they were palsied and sere--

4. And now, as the night was senescent/And star-dials pointed to morn--

5. At the end of our path a liquescent/And nebulous lustre was born,

6. Thus I pacified Psyche and kissed her,

7. And we passed to the end of the vista,

8. Then my heart it grew ashen and sober

Part II: Determining the Meaning -- Match the vocabulary words to their definitions.

___ 1. scoraic
___ 2. boreal
___ 3. sere
___ 4. senescent
___ 5. nebulous
___ 6. pacified
___ 7. vista
___ 8. ashen

A. Withered; dry
B. Cloudy, misty, or hazy
C. A distant view or prospect, especially one seen through an opening, as between rows of buildings
D. Growing old
E. To ease the anger or agitation of
F. North
G. Resembling ashes, especially in color; very pale
H. Porous cinderlike fragments of dark lava

Vocabulary - *The Bells*

Part I: Using Prior Knowledge and Contextual Clues

Below are the sentences in which the vocabulary words appear in the text. Read the sentence. Use any clues you can find in the sentence combined with your prior knowledge, and write what you think the underlined words mean on the lines provided.

1. What liquid <u>ditty</u> floats

_____

2-3. What a gush of <u>euphony</u> <u>voluminously</u> wells!

_____

_____

4. In a mad <u>expostulation</u> with the deaf and frantic fire,

_____

5. On the bosom of the <u>palpitating</u> air!

_____

6. At the melancholy <u>menace</u> of their tone!

_____

7. A <u>paean</u> from the bells!

_____

Part II: Determining the Meaning -- Match the vocabulary words to their definitions.

___ 1. ditty
___ 2. euphony
___ 3. voluminously
___ 4. expostulation
___ 5. palpitating
___ 6. menace
___ 7. paean

A. Agreeable sound
B. To reason earnestly with someone in an effort to dissuade or correct
C. A threat
D. Song of joyful praise
E. Quivering; throbbing
F. Having a great volume, fullness, size, or number
G. Little song

Vocabulary - *Annabel Lee*

Part I: Using Prior Knowledge and Contextual Clues

    Below are the sentences in which the vocabulary words appear in the text. Read the sentence. Use any clues you can find in the sentence combined with your prior knowledge, and write what you think the underlined words mean on the lines provided.

1-2. With a love that the winged seraphs of heaven/Coveted her and me.

_____

_____

3. To shut her up in a sepulchre

_____

4. The angels, not half so happy in heaven,/Went envying her and me--

_____

5. Nor the demons down under the sea,/Can ever dissever my soul from the soul

_____

Part II: Determining the Meaning -- Match the vocabulary words to their definitions.

   ___ 1. seraphs   A. A burial vault
   ___ 2. coveted   B. Separate
   ___ 3. sepulchre   C. A feeling of discontent and resentment
   ___ 4. envying   aroused by and in conjunction with
   ___ 5. dissever   desire for the possessions or qualities of
                                      another
                         D. Wished for longingly
                         E. Angels

ANSWER KEYS: PREREADING VOCABULARY WORKSHEETS
E. A. Poe Stories

Tell Tale Heart	Cask of Amontillado	Black Cat	Masque of Red Death
1. D	1. D	1. C	1. C
2. F	2. F	2. F	2. E
3. G	3. H	3. A	3. A
4. A	4. C	4. B	4. F
5. I	5. E	5. G	5. H
6. H	6. G	6. D	6. G
7. E	7. B	7. I	7. B
8. B	8. I	8. J	8. I
9. C	9. A	9. H	9. D
		10. E	

House of Usher	Rue Morgue		Purloined Letter
1. D	1. D	11. C	1. H
2. H	2. F	12. A	2. G
3. J	3. B	13. D	3. F
4. I	4. C	14. E	4. E
5. F	5. E	15. G	5. D
6. C	6. H	16. H	6. C
7. A	7. G	17. B	7. B
8. G	8. I	18. I	8. A
9. E	9. J	19. F	
10. B	10. A		

Pit and Pendulum	Raven	Lenore	To Helen	Ulalume
1. E	1. G	1. B	1. A	1. H
2. B	2. E	2. D	2. H	2. F
3. F	3. F	3. E	3. B	3. A
4. H	4. C	4. C	4. D	4. D
5. D	5. A	5. A	5. G	5. B
6. G	6. B		6. C	6. E
7. C	7. D		7. F	7. C
8. A			8. E	8. G

The Bells	Annabel Lee
1. G 5. E	1. E
2. A 6. C	2. D
3. F 7. D	3. A
4. B	4. C
	5. B

DAILY LESSONS

LESSON ONE

Objectives
1. To distribute the materials which will be used in the unit
2. To explain the group project students will do in this unit
3. To do the prereading vocabulary work for the horror story

NOTE: Prior to this lesson you need to have acquired a recording of either *The Black Cat* or *The Tell-Tale Heart*.

Activity #1
Darken your room to provide the appropriate atmosphere for a horror story. Play the recording of either *The Black Cat* or *The Tell-Tale Heart*.

TRANSITION: Explain that *The Black Cat* (or *The Tell-Tale Heart*) is an example of the horror stories written by Edgar Allan Poe. Other kinds of stories Poe wrote were gothic, detective, psychological thrillers, and stories about people with evil or double personalities. Poe also wrote quite a large number of poems.

Activity #2
Distribute the materials which will be used in this unit. Explain in detail how students are to use these materials.

Study Guides Students should read the study guide questions for each tale as homework the night before each tale is to be done in class to get a feeling for what events and ideas are important in the tale. After reading the section, students will as a class answer the questions to review the important events and ideas from that tale. Students should keep the study guides as study materials for the unit test.

Vocabulary Prior to listening to or reading each tale, students will do vocabulary work related to each tale. Following the completion of the reading of the text, there will be a vocabulary review of all the words used in the vocabulary assignments. Students should keep their vocabulary work as study materials for the unit test.

Reading Assignment Sheet You need to fill in the reading assignment sheet to let students know by when their presentations have to be completed. You can either write the assignment sheet on a side blackboard or bulletin board and leave it there for students to see each day, or you can "ditto" copies for each student to have. In either case, you should advise students to become very familiar with the reading assignments so they know what is expected of them.

  <u>Extra Activities Center</u> The Extra Activities page in this unit contains suggestions for an extra library of related books and articles in your classroom as well as crossword and word search puzzles. Make an extra activities center in your room where you will keep these materials for students to use. (Bring the books and articles in from the library and keep several copies of the puzzles on hand.) Explain to students that these materials are available for students to use when they finish reading assignments or other class work early or as extra review/study materials.

  <u>Nonfiction Assignment Sheet</u> Explain to students that they each are to read at least one non-fiction piece from the in-class library at some time during the unit. Suggest that students do this assignment in conjunction with the background research they will have to do for their presentations. Students will fill out a nonfiction assignment sheet after completing the reading to help you evaluate their reading experiences and to help the students think about and evaluate their own reading experiences.

  <u>Books</u> Each school has its own rules and regulations regarding student use of school books. Advise students of the procedures that are normal for your school.

<u>Activity #3</u>
  Show students how to preview the study questions and do the prereading vocabulary worksheets by doing the ones for the story you just listened to together in class. After these worksheets are completed, tell students they should read the text to the story you heard in class prior to your next class meeting.

NONFICTION ASSIGNMENT SHEET
(To be completed after reading the required nonfiction article)

Name _____ Date _____

Title of Nonfiction Read _____

Written By _____ Publication Date _____

I. Factual Summary: Write a short summary of the piece you read.

II. Vocabulary
    1. With which vocabulary words in the piece did you encounter some degree of difficulty?

    2. How did you resolve your lack of understanding with these words?

III. Interpretation: What was the main point the author wanted you to get from reading his work?

IV. Criticism
    1. With which points of the piece did you agree or find easy to accept? Why?

    2. With which points of the piece did you disagree or find difficult to believe? Why?

V. Personal Response: What do you think about this piece? OR How does this piece influence your ideas?

LESSON TWO

Objectives
1. To review the main ideas and events from the horror story the class heard and read
2. To preview the study questions and vocabulary for the gothic story students will read in the next class period

Activity #1
Give students a few minutes to formulate answers for the study guide questions for the horror story they read, and then discuss the answers to the questions in detail. Write the answers on the board or overhead transparency so students can have the correct answers for study purposes. Note: It is a good practice in public speaking and leadership skills for individual students to take charge of leading the discussions of the study questions. Perhaps a different student could go to the front of the class and lead the discussion each day that the study questions are discussed during this unit. Of course, the teacher should guide the discussion when appropriate and be sure to fill in any gaps the students leave.

Activity #2
Prior to your next class meeting, students should do the prereading work for the gothic tale (*The Fall of the House of Usher*). Students may use the remaining class time to begin this assignment.

LESSON THREE

Objectives
1. To read the gothic story *The Fall of the House of Usher*
2. To give students the opportunity to practice oral reading
3. To give the teacher the opportunity to evaluate students' oral reading

Activity
Have students read *The Fall of the House of Usher* out loud in class. You probably know the best way to get readers with your class; pick students at random, ask for volunteers, or use whatever method works best for your group. If you have not yet completed an oral reading evaluation for your students this marking period, this would be a good opportunity to do so. A form is included with this unit for your convenience.

ORAL READING EVALUATION - *Poe Stories*

Name _____ Class _____ Date _____

SKILL	EXCELLENT	GOOD	AVERAGE	FAIR	POOR
Fluency	5	4	3	2	1
Clarity	5	4	3	2	1
Audibility	5	4	3	2	1
Pronunciation	5	4	3	2	1
_____	5	4	3	2	1
_____	5	4	3	2	1

Total _____ Grade _____

Comments:

LESSON FOUR

Objectives
1. To review the main ideas and events of *The Fall of the House of Usher*
2. To do the prereading work for the detective stories students will read in their next class meeting
3. To make the poetry assignment

Activity #1
Give students a few minutes to formulate answers for the study guide questions for *The Fall of the House of Usher*, and then discuss the answers to the questions in detail. Write the answers on the board or overhead transparency so students can have the correct answers for study purposes.

Activity #2
Distribute the poetry assignment and the verse assignments. Discuss the directions in detail. Be sure to tell students the day/date that they will be required to make their presentations.

Activity #3
Tell students that prior to Lesson Six (give students a day/date) they should have completed the prereading work for the detective story they will read. If time remains in this class period, students may begin this assignment.

LESSON FIVE

Objectives
1. To give students the opportunity to practice writing to inform
2. To give the teacher the opportunity to evaluate students' writing skills
3. To review the Poe stories students have read
4. To show students the differences in the two types of stories they have read

Activity
Distribute Writing Assignment #1. Discuss the directions in detail and give students ample time to complete the assignment.

POETRY PROJECT - E. A. POE STORIES

ASSIGNMENT

You have been (or will soon be) assigned some lines of poetry from one of Poe's most well-know poems. All of you who have been assigned to work on the same poem will be asked to make a presentation about the poem in a couple of weeks. The presentation will be in two parts. You will say your poem lines (in order) from memory in front of the class, and then you will talk about the poem to the class including a summary of what happened in the poem/what the poem was about, a discussion about the "poetry" (rhyme, meter, word choice) of the poem, and a commentary giving your thoughts about the poem.

REQUIREMENTS

1. Each student must recite his/her lines from memory.
2. Each student must read the entire poem.
3. The length of the presentation will depend upon the length and content of the poem, but all presentations must be at least ten minutes long.
4. Each student in the group must complete Writing Assignment #2 prior to the group discussion of the poem.

GETTING STARTED

First, take the time to read the whole poem from start to finish.
Then, re-read the verses/lines you have been assigned.
Memorize your lines.
    Hints to help you memorize your lines:
        a. Write out your verses about ten times
        b. Practice saying your verses out loud so you can hear yourself say them
        c. Have a friend say the lines leaving out words for you to fill in
        d. Make flash cards--one for each line of poetry. Jumble them up and rearrange them to the correct order as often as you can.
        e. Make a recording of the verses and play it over and over again, at first listening and then saying the words with the recording.
In a paragraph or two, write out what happens in your poem or what your poem is about.
Make a list of the words that seem most important in the poem and make some notes about why you think they are important.
Look at how the poem is written -- the rhymes, the rhythms of the poem. What things do you notice about the author's word choice and the rhythms? Make some notes about your thoughts regarding these things.
When you get together in your group to discuss the poem, bring all of these things with you so you will all have something to discuss.

POEM VERSES ASSIGNMENTS - E. A. POE

Verse Assignment #	Student Name	Comments	Grade
1			
2			
3			
4			
5			
6			
7			
8			
9			
10			
11			
12			
13			
14			
15			
16			
17			
18			
19			
20			
21			
22			
23			
24			
25			
26			
27			
28			
29			

POEM VERSES

Assignment #1 : <u>The Raven</u>
Once upon a midnight dreary, while I pondered, weak and weary,
Over many a quaint and curious volume of forgotten lore --
While I nodded, nearly napping, suddenly there came a tapping,
As of some one gently rapping, rapping at my chamber door --
                Only this and nothing more.
Ah, distinctly I remember it was in the bleak December,
And each separate dying ember wrought its ghost upon the floor.
Eagerly I wished the morrow; -- vainly I had sought to borrow
From my books surcease of sorrow--sorrow for the lost Lenore--
For the rare and radiant maiden whom the angels name Lenore--
                Nameless here for evermore.

Assignment #2: <u>The Raven</u>
And the silken sad uncertain rustling of each purple curtain
Thrilled me--filled me with fantastic terrors never felt before;
So that now, to still the beating of my heart, I stood repeating:
"'Tis some visitor entreating entrance at my chamber door;
                This it is and nothing more."
Presently my soul grew stronger; hesitating then no longer,
"Sir." said I, "or Madam, truly your forgiveness I implore;
But the fact is I was napping, and so gently you came rapping,
And so faintly you came tapping, tapping at my chamber door,
That I scarce was sure I heard you" --here I opened wide the door; --
                Darkness there and nothing more.

Assignment #3: <u>The Raven</u>
Deep into that darkness peering, long I stood there wondering, fearing,
Doubting, dreaming dreams no mortals ever dared to dream before;
But the silence was unbroken, and the stillness gave no token,
And the only word there spoken was the whispered word, "Lenore!"
This I whispered, and an echo murmured back the word, "Lenore!" --
                Merely this and nothing more.
Back into the chamber turning, all my soul within me burning,
Soon again I heard a tapping somewhat louder than before.
"Surely," said I, "surely that is something at my window lattice;
Let me see, then what thereat is, and this mystery explore --
Let my heart be still a moment, and this mystery explore; --
                'Tis the wind and nothing more."

Assignment #4: The Raven
Open here I flung the shutter, when, with many a flirt and flutter,
In there stepped a stately Raven of the saintly days of yore.
Not the least obeisance made he; not a minute stopped or stayed he,
But, with mien of lord or lady, perched above my chamber door --
Perched upon a bust of Pallas just above my chamber door --
      Perched, and sat, and nothing more.
Then this ebony bird beguiling my sad fancy into smiling,
By the grave and stern decorum of the countenance it wore,
"Though thy crest be shorn and shaven, thou," I said, "art sure no craven,
Ghastly grim and ancient Raven wandering from the Nightly shore!"
Tell me what thy lordly name is on the Night's Plutonian shore!"
      Quoth the Raven, "Nevermore."

Assignment #5: The Raven
Much I marvelled this ungainly fowl to hear discourse so plainly,
Though its answer little meaning -- little relevancy bore;
For we cannot help agreeing that no living human being
Ever yet was blessed with seeing bird above his chamber door--
Bird or beast upon the sculptured bust above his chamber door,
      With such name as "Nevermore."
But the Raven, sitting lonely on that placid bust, spoke only
That one word, as if his soul in that one word he did outpour.
Nothing farther then he uttered; not a feather then he fluttered--
Till I scarcely more than muttered: "Other friends have flown before --
On the morrow he will leave me as my Hopes have flown before."
      Then the bird said, "Nevermore."

Assignment #6: The Raven
Startled at the stillness broken by reply so aptly spoken,
"Doubtless," said I, "what it utters is its only stock and store,
Caught from some unhappy master whom unmerciful Disaster
Followed fast and followed faster till his songs one burden bore --
Till the dirges of his Hope that melancholy burden bore
      One of 'Never--nevermore."
But the Raven still beguiling all my sad soul into smiling,
Straight I wheeled a cushioned seat in front of bird and bust and door;
Then, upon the velvet sinking, I betook myself to linking
Fancy unto fancy, thinking what this ominous bird of yore --
What this grim, ungainly, ghastly, gaunt, and ominous bird or yore
      Meant in croaking "Nevermore."

Assignment #7: The Raven
This I sat engaged in guessing, but no syllable expressing
To the fowl whose fiery eyes now burned into my bosom's core;
This and more I sat divining, with my head at ease reclining
On the cushion's velvet lining that the lamp-light gloated o'er,
But whose velvet violet lining with the lamp-light gloating o'er
    She shall press, ah, nevermore!
Then, methought, the air grew denser, perfumed from an unseen censer
Swung by Seraphim whose foot-falls tinkled on the tufted floor.
"Wretch," I cried, "thy God hath lent thee -- by these angels he hath sent thee
Respite--respite and nepenthe from thy memories of Lenore!
Quaff, oh quaff this kind nepenthe and forget this lost Lenore!"
    Quoth the Raven, "Nevermore."

Assignment #8: The Raven
"Prophet!" said I, "thing of evil! -- prophet still, if bird or devil! --
Whether Tempter sent, or whether tempest tossed thee here ashore,
Desolate, yet all undaunted, on this desert land enchanted --
On this home by Horror haunted, -- tell me truly, I implore --
Is there -- is there balm in Gilead?--tell me--tell me, I implore!"
    Quoth the Raven, "Nevermore."
"Prophet!" said I, "thing of evil! -- prophet still, if bird or devil!
By that heaven that bends above us -- by that God we both adore --
Tell this soul with sorrow laden if, within the distant Aidenn,
It shall clasp a sainted maiden whom the angels name Lenore --
Clasp a rare and radiant maiden whom the angels name Lenore."
    Quoth the Raven, "Nevermore."

Assignment #9: The Raven
"Be that word our sign of parting, bird or fiend!" I shrieked, upstarting --
"Get thee back into the tempest and the Night's Plutonian shore!
Leave no black plume as a token of that lie thy soul hath spoken!
Leave my loneliness unbroken!--quit the bust above my door!
Take thy beak from out my heart, and take thy form from off my door!"
    Quoth the Raven, "Nevermore."
And the Raven, never flitting, still is sitting, still is sitting
On the pallid bust of Pallas just above my chamber door;
And his eyes have all the seeming of a demon's that is dreaming,
And the lamp-light o'er him streaming throws his shadow on the floor;
And my soul from out that shadow that lies floating on the floor
    Shall be lifted -- nevermore!

Assignment #10: <u>Lenore</u>
Ah, broken is the golden bowl! the spirit flown forever!
Let the bell toll! -- a saintly soul floats on the Stygian river;
And, Guy De Vere, has thou no tear? -- weep now or never more!
See on yon drear and rigid bier low lies thy love, Lenore!
Come! let the burial rite be read -- the funeral song be sung! --
An anthem for the queenliest dead that ever died so young --
A dirge for her the doubly dead in that she died so young.

"Wretches! ye loved her for her wealth and hated her for her pride,
And when she fell in feeble health, ye blessed her -- that she died!
How shall the ritual, then, be read? -- the requiem how be sung
By you -- by yours, the evil eye, -- by yours, the slanderous tongue
That did to death the innocence that died, and died so young?

Assignment #11: <u>Lenore</u>
Peccavimus; but rave not thus! and let a Sabbath song
Go up to God so solemnly the dead may feel no wrong!
The sweet Lenore hath "gone before," with Hope, that flew beside,
Leaving thee wild for the dear child that should have been thy bride --
For her, the fair and debonair, that now so lowly lies,
The life upon her yellow hair but not within her eyes --
The life still there, upon her hair -- the death upon her eyes.

Avaunt! to-night my heart is light. No dirge will I upraise,
But waft the angel on her flight with a paean of old days!
Let no bell toll! -- lest her sweet soul, amid its hallowed mirth,
Should catch the note, as it doth float up from the damned Earth.
To friends above, from fiends below, the indignant ghost is riven --
From Hell unto a high estate far up within the Heaven --
From grief and groan, to a golden throne, beside the King of Heaven.

Assignment #12: <u>To Helen</u>
I saw thee once -- once only -- years ago;
I must not say how many -- but not many.
It was a July midnight; and from out
A full-orbed moon, that, like thine own soul, soaring,
Sought a precipitate pathway up through heaven,
There fell a silvery-silken veil of light,
With quietude, and sultriness, and slumber,
Upon the upturn'd faces of a thousand
Roses that grew in an enchanted garden,
Where no wind dared to stir, unless on tiptoe --
Fell on the upturn'd faces of these roses
That gave out, in return for the love-light,
Their odorous souls in an ecstatic death --
Fell on the upturn'd faces of these roses
That smiled and died in this parterre, enchanted
By thee, and by the poetry of thy presence.
Clad all in white, upon a violet bank
I saw thee half reclining; while the moon
Fell on the upturn'd faces of the roses,
And on thine own, upturn'd -- alas, in sorrow!

Assignment #13: <u>To Helen</u>
Was it not Fate that, on this July midnight --
Was it not Fate (whose name is also Sorrow),
That bade me pause before that garden-gate,
To breathe the incense of those slumbering roses?
No footsteps stirred; the hated world all slept,
Save only thee and me. (Oh, Heaven! -- oh, God!
How my heart beats in coupling those two words!)
Save only thee and me. I paused -- I looked --
And in an instant all things disappeared.
(Ah, bear in mind this garden was enchanted!)

Assignment #14: To Helen
The pearly lustre of the moon went out;
The mossy banks and the meandering paths,
The happy flowers and the repining trees,
Were seen no more: the very roses' odors
Died in the arms of the adoring airs.
All -- all expired save thee -- save less than thou:
Save only the divine light in thine eyes --
Save but the soul in thine uplifted eyes.
I saw but them -- they were the world to me.
I saw but them -- saw only them for hours--
Saw only them until the moon went down.
What wild heart-histories seemed to lie enwritten
Upon those crystalline, celestial spheres!
How dark a woe! yet how sublime a hope!
How silently serene a sea of pride!
How daring an ambition! yet how deep --
How fathomless a capacity for love!

Assignment #15: To Helen
But now, at length, dear Dian sank from sight,
Into a western couch of thunder-cloud;
And thou, a ghost, amid the entombing trees
Didst glide away. Only thine eyes remained.
They would not go -- they never yet have gone.
Lighting my lonely pathway home that night,
They have not left me (as my hopes have) since.

They follow me -- they lead me through the years.
They are my ministers -- yet I their slave.
Their office is to illumine and enkindle --
My duty, to be saved by their bright light,
And purified in their electric fire,
And sanctified in their Elysian fire.
They fill my soul with Beauty (which is Hope),
And are far up in heaven -- the stars I kneel to
In the sad, silent watches of my night;
While even in the meridian glare of day
I see them still -- two sweetly scintillant
Venuses, unextinguished by the sun!

Assignment #16: Ulalume
The skies they were ashen and sober;
    The leaves they were crisped and sere --
    The leaves they were withering and sere;
It was night in the lonesome October
    Of my most immemorial year;
It was hard by the dim lake of Auber,
    In the misty mid region of Weir --
It was down by the dank tarn of Auber,
    In the ghoul-haunted woodland of Weir.

Here once, through an alley Titanic,
    Of cypress, I roamed with my Soul --
    Of cypress, with Psyche, my Soul.
These were days when my heart was volcanic
    As the scoric rivers that roll --
    As the lavas that restlessly roll
Their sulphurous currents down Yaanek
    In the ultimate climes of the pole --
That groan as they roll down Mount Yaanek
    In the realms of the boreal pole.

Assignment #17: Ulalume
Our talk had been serious and sober,
    But our thoughts they were palsied and sere --
    Our memories were treacherous and sere, --
For we knew not the month was October,
    And we marked not the night of the year --
    (Ah, night of all nights in the year!)
We noted not the dim lake of Auber --
    (Though once we had jouneyed down here) --
Remembered not the dank tarn of Auber,
    Nor the ghoul-haunted woodland of Weir.

And now, as the night was senescent
    And star-dials pointed to morn --
    As the star-dials hinted of morn --
At the end of our path a liquescent
    And nebulous lustre was born,
Out of which a miraculous crescent
    Arose with a duplicate horn --
Astarte's bediamonded crescent
    Distinct with its duplicate horn.

Assignment #18: <u>Ulalume</u>

And I said: "She is warmer than Dian;
        She rolls through an ether of sighs --
        She revels in a region of sighs:
She has seen that the tears are not dry on
        These cheeks, where the worm never dies,
And has come past the stars of the Lion
        To point us the path to the skies
        To the Lethean peace of the skies --
Come up, in despite of the Lion,
        To shine on us with her bright eyes --
Come up through the lair of the Lion,
        With love in her luminous eyes."

But Psyche, uplifting her finger,
        Said: "Sadly this star I mistrust --
        Her pallor I strangely mistrust: --
Oh, hasten! -- oh, let us not linger!
        Oh, fly! -- let us fly! -- for we must."
In terror she spoke, letting sink her
        Wings until they trailed in the dust --
In agony sobbed, letting sink her
        Plumes till they trailed in the dust --
        Till they sorrowfully trailed in the dust.

Assignment #19: <u>Ulalume</u>

I replied: "This is nothing but dreaming:
    Let us on by this tremulous light!
    Let us bathe in this crystalline light!
Its Sibyllic splendor is beaming
    With Hope and in Beauty to-night! --
    See! -- it flickers up the sky through the night!
Ah, we safely may trust to its gleaming,
    And be sure it will lead us aright --
We safely may trust to a gleaming,
    That cannot but guide us aright,
    Since it flickers up to Heaven through the night."

Thus I pacified Psyche and kissed her,
    And tempted her out of her gloom--
    And conquered her scruples and gloom;
And we passed to the end of the vista,
    But were stopped by the door of a tomb --
    By the door of a legended tomb;
And I said: "What is written, sweet sister,
    On the door of this legended tomb?
    She replied: "Ulalume -- Ulalume --
    'Tis the vault of thy lost Ulalume!"

Assignment #20: <u>Ulalume</u>
Then my heart it grew ashen and sober
      As the leaves that were crisped and sere --
      As the leaves that were withering and sere,
And I cried: "It was surely October
      On this very night of last year
          That I journeyed -- I journeyed down here --
          That I brought a dread burden down here --
      On this night of all nights in the year,
      Ah, what demon has tempted me here?
Well I know, now, this dim lake of Auber --
      This misty mid region of Weir --
Well I know, now, this dank tarn of Auber,
      This ghoul-haunted woodland of Weir."

Assignment #21: <u>The Bells</u>
      Hear the sledges with the bells--
          Silver bells!
What a world of merriment their melody foretells!
      How they tinkle, tinkle, tinkle,
          In the icy air of night!
      While the stars that oversprinkle
      All the heavens seems to twinkle
          With a crystalline delight;
      Keeping time, time, time
      In a sort of Runic rhyme,
To the tintinnabulation that so musically wells
      From the bells, bells, bells, bells
          Bells, bells, bells --
From the jingling and the tinkling of the bells.

      Hear the mellow wedding bells,
          Golden bells!
What a world of happiness their harmony foretells!
      Through the balmy air of night
      How they ring out their delight!
      From the molten-golden notes,
          And all in tune,
      What a liquid ditty floats
To the turtle-dove that listens, while she gloats
          On the moon!

Assignment #22: <u>The Bells</u>
>Oh, from out the sounding cells
What a gush of euphony voluminously wells!
>>How it swells!
>>How it dwells
>On the Future! how it tells
>Of the rapture that impels
>To the swinging and the ringing of the bells, bells, bells,
>Of the bells, bells, bells, bells,
>>Bells, bells, bells --
To the rhyming and the chiming of the bells!

- -

Assignment #23: <u>The Bells</u>
>Hear the loud alarum bells--
>>Brazen bells!
What a tale of terror, now, their turbulency tells!
>In the startled ear of night
>How they scream out their affright!
>Too much horrified to speak,
>They can only shriek, shriek,
>>Out of tune,
In a clamourous appealing to the mercy of the fire,
In a mad expostulation with the deaf and frantic fire,
>Leaping higher, higher, higher,
>With a desperate desire,
>And a resolute endeavor
>Now -- now to sit, or never,
>By the side of the pale-faced moon.
>Oh, the bells, bells, bells!
>What a tale their terror tells
>>Of despair!
>How they clang, and clash, and roar!
>What a horror they outpour
On the bosom of the palpitating air!

Assignment #24: <u>The Bells</u>
      Yet the ear it fully knows,
           By the twanging,
           And the clanging,
    How the danger ebbs and flows;
    Yet the ear distinctly tells,
         In the jangling,
         And the wrangling,
   How the danger sinks and swells,
By the sinking or the swelling in the anger of the bells --
        Of the bells --
   Of the bells, bells, bells, bells,
      Bells, bells, bells --
In the clamor and the clangor of the bells!

Assignment #25: <u>The Bells</u>
     Hear the tolling of the bells --
        Iron bells!
What a world of solemn thought their melody compels!
     In the silence of the night,
     How we shiver with affright
     At the melancholy menace of their tone
     For every sound that floats
     From the rust within their throats
       Is a groan.
     And the people--ah, the people--
     They that dwell up in the steeple,
        All alone,
     And who tolling, tolling, tolling,
      In that muffled monotone,
     Feel a glory in so rolling
      On the human heart a stone --
     They are neither man nor woman --
     They are neither brute nor human --
        They are Ghouls:

Assignment #26: The Bells

      And their king it is who tolls;
      And he rolls, rolls, rolls,
          Rolls
      A paean from the bells!
      And his merry bosom swells
      With the paean of the bells!
      And he dances, and he yells;
      Keeping time, time time,
      In a sort of Runic rhyme,
        To the paean of the bells --
          Of the bells:
      Keeping time, time time,
      In a sort of Runic rhyme,
        To the throbbing of the bells --
      Of the bells, bells, bells--
        To the sobbing of the bells;
      Keeping time, time, time,
        As he knells, knells, knells,
      In a happy Runic rhyme,
        To the rolling of the bells --
      Of the bells, bells, bells --
        To the tolling of the bells,
Of the bells, bells, bells, bells --
          Bells, bells, bells --
To the moaning and the groaning of the bells.

Assignment #27: <u>Annabel Lee</u>
It was many and many a year ago,
      In a kingdom by the sea,
That a maiden there lived whom you may know
      By the name of ANNABEL LEE;
And this maiden she lived with no other thought
      Than to love and be loved by me.

I was a child and she was a child,
      In this kingdom by the sea:
But we loved with a love that was more than love --
      I and my ANNABEL LEE;
With a love that the winged seraphs of heaven
      Coveted her and me.

Assignment #28: <u>Annabel Lee</u>
And this was the reason that, long ago,
      In this kingdom by the sea,
A wind blew out of a cloud, chilling
      My beautiful ANNABEL LEE;
So that her high-born kinsman came
      And bore her away from me,
To shut her up in a sepulchre
      In this kingdom by the sea.

The angels, not half so happy in heaven,
      Went envying her and me --
Yes! -- that was the reason (as all men know,
      In this kingdom by the sea)
That the wind came out of the cloud by night,
      Chilling and killing my ANNABEL LEE.

Assignment #29: <u>Annabel Lee</u>
But our love it was stronger by far than the love
      Of those who were older than we --
      Of many far wiser than we --
And neither the angels in heaven above,
      Nor the demons down under the sea,
Can ever dissever my soul from the soul
      Of the beautiful ANNABEL LEE.

For the moon never beams, without bringing me dreams
      Of the beautiful ANNABEL LEE;
And the stars never rise, but I feel the bright eyes
      Of the beautiful ANNABEL LEE;
And so, all the night-tide, I lie down by the side
Of my darling -- my darling -- my life and my bride,
      In the sepulchre there by the sea,
      In her tomb by the sounding sea.

WRITING ASSIGNMENT #1 - E. A. POE STORIES

PROMPT
  Poe was fond of using the first person narrator to tell his stories. Your assignment is to compare his use of the narrator in the first two stories we have read.

PREWRITING
  One way to start is to stop and think about Poe's use of the narrator in each story. List characteristics of the narrator in the first story and jot down notes about his function in the story. Now do the same for the second story.
  Take a minute to compare your two lists and your notes. Think about the similarities and differences. Think of one statement which will summarize the conclusions you have come to after looking at your data. That will be the main idea of your paper, your thesis.

DRAFTING
  Write an introductory paragraph in which you introduce the fact that Poe used the first person narrator and work your way around to stating your thesis.
  In the body of your composition, write one paragraph telling about the narrator in the first story you read, and then write another paragraph telling about the narrator in the second story you read.
  Your concluding paragraph should summarize your ideas and give your final thoughts on the topic.

PROMPT
  When you finish the rough draft of your paper, ask a student who sits near you to read it. After reading your rough draft, he/she should tell you what he/she liked best about your work, which parts were difficult to understand, and ways in which your work could be improved. Reread your paper considering your critic's comments, and make the corrections you think are necessary.

PROOFREADING
  Do a final proofreading of your paper double-checking your grammar, spelling, organization, and the clarity of your ideas.

LESSON SIX

Objectives
1. To read *The Murder in the Rue Morgue* or *The Purloined Letter*
2. To give students the opportunity to practice oral reading
3. To give the teacher the opportunity to evaluate students' oral reading

Activity
Have students read detective story of your choice aloud in class. You probably know the best way to get readers with your class; pick students at random, ask for volunteers, or use whatever method works best for your group. If you have not yet completed an oral reading evaluation for your students this marking period, this would be a good opportunity to do so. A form is included with this unit for your convenience.

LESSON SEVEN

Objectives
1. To review the main ideas and events from the detective story the class read
2. To preview the study questions and vocabulary for the psychological story students will read in the next class period

Activity #1
Give students a few minutes to formulate answers for the study guide questions for the detective story they read, and then discuss the answers to the questions in detail. Write the answers on the board or overhead transparency so students can have the correct answers for study purposes.

Activity #2
Prior to your next class meeting, students should do the prereading work for the psychological tale of your choice. Students may use the remaining class time to begin this assignment.

LESSON EIGHT

Objectives
1. To read *The Pit and the Pendulum* or *The Masque of Red Death*
2. To give students the opportunity to practice oral reading
3. To give the teacher the opportunity to evaluate students' oral reading

Activity

Have students read psychological story of your choice aloud in class. You probably know the best way to get readers with your class; pick students at random, ask for volunteers, or use whatever method works best for your group. If you have not yet completed an oral reading evaluation for your students this marking period, this would be a good opportunity to do so. A form is included with this unit for your convenience.

LESSON NINE

Objectives
1. To review the main ideas and events from the psychological story the class read
2. To preview the study questions and vocabulary for *The Cask of Amontillado*

Activity #1

Give students a few minutes to formulate answers for the study guide questions for the psychological story they read, and then discuss the answers to the questions in detail. Write the answers on the board or overhead transparency so students can have the correct answers for study purposes.

Activity #2

Prior to your next class meeting, students should do the prereading work for *The Cask of Amontillado*. Students may use the remaining class time to begin this assignment.

LESSON TEN

Objectives
   1. To read *The Cask of Amontillado*
   2. To give students the opportunity to practice oral reading
   3. To give the teacher the opportunity to evaluate students' oral reading

Activity

   Have students read *The Cask of Amontillado* aloud in class. You probably know the best way to get readers with your class; pick students at random, ask for volunteers, or use whatever method works best for your group. If you have not yet completed an oral reading evaluation for your students this marking period, this would be a good opportunity to do so. A form is included with this unit for your convenience.

LESSON ELEVEN

Objectives
   1. To review the main ideas and events from *The Cask of Amontillado*
   2. To review and discuss in more depth all the stories included in this unit

Activity #1

   Give students a few minutes to formulate answers for the study guide questions for *The Cask of Amontillado* , and then discuss the answers to the questions in detail. Write the answers on the board or overhead transparency so students can have the correct answers for study purposes.

Activity #2

   Choose the questions from the Extra Discussion Questions/Writing Assignments which seem most appropriate for your students. A class discussion of these questions is most effective if students have been given the opportunity to formulate answers to the questions prior to the discussion. To this end, you may either have all the students formulate answers to all the questions, divide your class into groups and assign one or more questions to each group, or you could assign one question to each student in your class. The option you choose will make a difference in the amount of class time needed for this activity.

   After students have had ample time to formulate answers to the questions, begin your class discussion of the questions and the ideas presented by the questions. Be sure students take notes during the discussion so they have information to study for the unit test.

EXTRA WRITING ASSIGNMENTS/DISCUSSION QUESTIONS - *Poe Stories*

<u>Interpretation</u>

1. From what point of view are most of Poe's stories written? What effect does this have on the total work?

2. What do the settings of Poe's stories contribute to the stories?

3. Tell where the climax is in each of the Poe stories you have read.

4. Are the characters in Poe Stories stereotypes? If so, explain why Edgar Allan Poe used stereotypes. If not, explain how the characters merit individuality.

<u>Critical</u>

5. Characterize Edgar Allan Poe's style of writing. How does it contribute to the value of the work?

6. What possible significance could there be in the fact Red Death travels from the East (blue) room to the West (black) room?

7. Explain the symbolic importance of the crack in *The Fall of the House of Usher*

8. Are Poe's stories believable? Why or why not? Discuss "the willing suspension of disbelief."

9. What symbolic inferences could be drawn if Lady Madeline (in *Usher*) was never alive when the narrator caught a glimpse of her?

10. What does the vague setting add to Poe's stories?

11. Compare the narrators of Poe's stories.

12. Give the main characteristics of the five different kinds of stories Poe wrote.

<u>Personal Response</u>

13. Did you enjoy reading *Poe Stories*? Why or why not?

14. Which of Poe's characters did you think was the most evil? Why?

15. Which of Poe's stories did you like the best? Why?

LESSON TWELVE

Objective
	To review the vocabulary words chosen for this unit

Activity
	Choose one of the vocabulary review activities listed below and spend your class time as directed. Some of the materials for these review activities are located in the Vocabulary Resource Materials section in this unit.

NOTE: Students are not being held responsible for all of the vocabulary words from all of the vocabulary worksheets. We have chosen 47 of the 114 words students reviewed for the stories.

LESSON THIRTEEN

Objectives
	1. To help students prepare for the poetry presentations
	2. To give students the opportunity to practice writing to inform
	3. To give the teacher the opportunity to evaluate students' writing

Activity
	Distribute Writing Assignment #2. Discuss the directions in detail and give students ample time to complete the assignment.

LESSON FOURTEEN

Objectives
	1. To give students time to meet in their poetry groups to discuss their poems and their notes
	2. To give students time to prepare their poetry presentations

Activity
	During this class period, students should meet in their poem groups to discuss their notes and plan their presentations. They should also practice their oral presentation of the poem. Students should also decide among themselves who will make the different parts of the presentations to the class.

VOCABULARY LIST - E. A. POE STORIES

These are the vocabulary words from which your vocabulary test will be taken.

AMID	In the middle of
ANNIHILATE	To reduce to nonexistence; to nullify or render void; abolish
APPARITION	A ghostly figure
ASCERTAIN	To find out
ASTUTE	Shrewd
ASUNDER	Into separate parts or pieces
AUDACITY	Boldness; daring
BEGUILING	Deceiving; diverting
COGNIZANT	Aware; familiar with
CONCEIVED	To form or develop in the mind; devise
CONSIGNED	Handed over
CORROBORATES	To strengthen or support with other evidence
COUNTENANCES	Faces
COVETED	Wished for longingly
CULPABLE	Responsible; at fault
DERISION	Scoffing; ridicule
DISSIMULATION	Concealing one's true feelings or intentions
ECSTATIC	Euphoric; blissful
EGREGIOUS	Bad or offensive
EGRESS	Exit; escape
ENAMORED	Inspired; captivated
EPOCH	Age; time
IMPEDED	Obstructed
IMPUNITY	Exemption from punishment, penalty, or harm
IRREVOCABLE	Can't be turned back
LIVID	Bruised
LUCID	Easily understood; sane or rational
MALEVOLENCE	Ill will toward others; rancor; malice; evil influence, especially supernatural
MANIFOLD	One of many kinds
MIEN	Manner
NEBULOUS	Cloudy, misty, or hazy
ODIOUS	Evoking feelings of repulsion
ORBS	Eyes
PALLID	Pale; dull
PERVERSENESS	Quality of being directed away from what is right or good; an appalling action, situation or object
PRODIGIOUS	Enormous
PROMISCUOUSLY	Casually; randomly
REQUIEM	A hymn, composition, or service for the dead
SAGACIOUS	Wise
SAGACITY	The quality of being discerning, sound in judgment
SERE	Withered; dry
SUBLIME	Majestic; inspiring awe; impressive
SUCCUMBED	Gave in
SULTRINESS	Sensualness; voluptuousness
UNPERCEIVED	Unnoticed
VEXED	To bring distress or suffering to; plague
VORACITY	Wild hunger

VOCABULARY REVIEW ACTIVITIES

1. Divide your class into two teams and have an old-fashioned spelling or definition bee.

2. Give each of your students (or students in groups of two, three or four) a *Poe Stories* Vocabulary Word Search Puzzle. The person (group) to find all of the vocabulary words in the puzzle first wins.

3. Give students a *Poe Stories* Vocabulary Word Search Puzzle without the word list. The person or group to find the most vocabulary words in the puzzle wins.

4. Use a *Poe Stories* Vocabulary Crossword Puzzle. Put the puzzle onto a transparency on the overhead projector (so everyone can see it), and do the puzzle together as a class.

5. Give students a *Poe Stories* Vocabulary Matching Worksheet to do.

6. Divide your class into two teams. Use *Poe Stories* vocabulary words with their letters jumbled as a word list. Student 1 from Team A faces off against Student 1 from Team B. You write the first jumbled word on the board. The first student (1A or 1B) to unscramble the word wins the chance for his/her team to score points. If 1A wins the jumble, go to student 2A and give him/her a definition. He/she must give you the correct spelling of the vocabulary word which fits that definition. If he/she does, Team A scores a point, and you give student 3A a definition for which you expect a correctly spelled matching vocabulary word. Continue giving Team A definitions until some team member makes an incorrect response. An incorrect response sends the game back to the jumbled-word face off, this time with students 2A and 2B. Instead of repeating giving definitions to the first few students of each team, continue with the student after the one who gave the last incorrect response on the team. For example, if Team B wins the jumbled-word face-off, and student 5B gave the last incorrect answer for Team B, you would start this round of definition questions with student 6B, and so on. The team with the most points wins!

7. Have students write a story in which they correctly use as many vocabulary words as possible. Have students read their compositions orally! Post the most original compositions on your bulletin board!

WRITING ASSIGNMENT #2 - E. A. Poe Stories

PROMPT
During your next class meeting, you will be getting together with other students who have been working on the same poem you have been. When you get together, you will be planning your presentation of the poem to the class and discussing your own reflections on the poem. Just to make sure your own thoughts are in order before you enter the group discussion, you should write down your own thoughts about the poem for the presentation.

Your assignment is to write a composition in which you give your own thoughts about the poem based on the requirements for the presentation.

PREWRITING
Look at your Poetry Project assignment sheet in the first paragraph labeled "assignment." Besides the oral reading of the poem, which you should have been working on all along, you will also have to give a summary of the poem, a discussion of the "poetry" of the poem, and a commentary giving your thoughts about the poem. Focus your Writing Assignment #2 on the last three parts just mentioned. Make some notes telling what the poem is about. Then, go back and look at the poem, paying particular attention to the meter, rhyme, and word choice. Make notes about what you observe. Finally, jot down some notes giving your thoughts about the poem.

DRAFTING
Your Writing Assignment #2 will have five parts, each with its own heading: "Poem Summary," "Meter," "Rhyme," "Word Choice," and "Commentary." Use your notes to write about each of these headings relating to your poem. Your writing should be in paragraph form.

PROMPT
When you finish the rough draft of your paper, ask a student who sits near you to read it. After reading your rough draft, he/she should tell you what he/she liked best about your work, which parts were difficult to understand, and ways in which your work could be improved. Reread your paper considering your critic's comments, and make the corrections you think are necessary.

PROOFREADING
Do a final proofreading of your paper double-checking your grammar, spelling, organization, and the clarity of your ideas.

LESSONS FIFTEEN AND SIXTEEN

Objectives
1. To discuss the poetry of Edgar Allan Poe
2. To bring the poetry project to a close
3. To give students the opportunity to make their poetry presentations

Activity
Have the poetry groups make their presentations to the class. The amount of time this activity will take will vary depending on the ability level of your students; we have allowed two class periods.

LESSON SEVENTEEN

Objectives
1. To widen the breadth of students' knowledge about the topics discussed or touched upon in the Poe stories
2. To check students' nonfiction reading assignments

Activity
Ask each student to give a brief oral report about the nonfiction work he/she read for the nonfiction reading assignment. Your criteria for evaluating this report will vary depending on the level of your students. You may wish for students to give a complete report without using notes of any kind, or you may want students to read directly from a written report, or you may want to do something in between these two extremes. Just make students aware of your criteria in ample time for them to prepare their reports.

Start with one student's report. After that, ask if anyone else in the class has read on a topic related to the first student's report. If no one has, choose another student at random. After each report, be sure to ask if anyone has a report related to the one just completed. That will help keep a continuity during the discussion of the reports.

LESSON EIGHTEEN

Objectives
1. To give students the opportunity to practice writing to persuade
2. To help students review the main ideas from *Poe Stories*

Activity
Distribute Writing Assignment #3. Discuss the directions in detail and give students ample time to complete the assignment.

While students are doing the assignment, call individual students to your desk or some other private area to have individual writing conferences using writing assignments one and two as the basis for your discussion. An evaluation form is included with this unit for your convenience.

LESSON NINETEEN

Objective
To review the main ideas presented in *Poe Stories*

Activity
Choose one of the review games/activities included in the packet and spend your class period as outlined there. Some materials for these activities are located in the Extra Activities Packet section of this unit.

WRITING ASSIGNMENT #3 - *Poe Stories*

PROMPT
Your assignment is to write a composition in which you make persuasive arguments that Poe was, indeed, a talented writer of fiction worth reading.

PREWRITING
Make a list of things that make fiction worth reading. Which of these characteristics does Poe's work reflect? Add to your list anything Poe had to offer in addition to the characteristics you have already noted. What were his strengths as a writer? Next to each item on your list, write down several specific examples from the works of Poe we have read.

DRAFTING
Write a paragraph in which you introduce the idea that Poe was a talented writer of fiction worth reading.

Write one paragraph for each of the characteristics you have noted on your list. In each paragraph, use specific examples to support your topic sentence.

Write a concluding paragraph in which you bring your composition to a close and give your final thoughts on the topic.

PROMPT
When you finish the rough draft of your paper, ask a student who sits near you to read it. After reading your rough draft, he/she should tell you what he/she liked best about your work, which parts were difficult to understand, and ways in which your work could be improved. Reread your paper considering your critic's comments, and make the corrections you think are necessary.

PROOFREADING
Do a final proofreading of your paper double-checking your grammar, spelling, organization, and the clarity of your ideas.

WRITING EVALUATION FORM - *Poe Stories*

Name _____ Date _____

Writing Assignment #1 for *Poe Stories* unit   Grade _____

Circle One For Each Item:

Grammar: correct   errors noted on paper

Spelling: correct   errors noted on paper

Punctuation: correct   errors noted on paper

Legibility: excellent   good   fair   poor

Strengths:

Weaknesses:

Comments/Suggestions:

REVIEW GAMES/ACTIVITIES - *Poe Stories*

1. Ask the class to make up a unit test for *Poe Stories*. The test should have 4 sections: matching, true/false, short answer, and essay. Students may use 1/2 period to make the test and then swap papers and use the other 1/2 class period to take a test a classmate has devised. (open book) You may want to use the unit test included in this packet or take questions from the students' unit tests to formulate your own test.

2. Take 1/2 period for students to make up true and false questions (including the answers). Collect the papers and divide the class into two teams. Draw a big tic-tac-toe board on the chalk board. Make one team X and one team O. Ask questions to each side, giving each student one turn. If the question is answered correctly, that students' team's letter (X or O) is placed in the box. If the answer is incorrect, no mark is placed in the box. The object is to get three marks in a row like tic-tac-toe. You may want to keep track of the number of games won for each team.

3. Take 1/2 period for students to make up questions (true/false and short answer). Collect the questions. Divide the class into two teams. You'll alternate asking questions to individual members of teams A & B (like in a spelling bee). The question keeps going from A to B until it is correctly answered, then a new question is asked. A correct answer does not allow the team to get another question. Correct answers are +2 points; incorrect answers are -1 point.

4. Have students pair up and quiz each other from their study guides and class notes.

5. Give students a *Poe Stories* crossword puzzle to complete.

6. Divide your class into two teams. Use *Poe Stories* crossword words with their letters jumbled as a word list. Student 1 from Team A faces off against Student 1 from Team B. You write the first jumbled word on the board. The first student (1A or 1B) to unscramble the word wins the chance for his/her team to score points. If 1A wins the jumble, go to student 2A and give him/her a clue. He/she must give you the correct word which matches that clue. If he/she does, Team A scores a point, and you give student 3A a clue for which you expect another correct response. Continue giving Team A clues until some team member makes an incorrect response. An incorrect response sends the game back to the jumbled-word face off, this time with students 2A and 2B. Instead of repeating giving clues to the first few students of each team, continue with the student after the one who gave the last incorrect response on the team. For example, if Team B wins the jumbled-word face-off, and student 5B gave the last incorrect answer for Team B, you would start this round of clue questions with student 6B, and so on. The team with the most points wins!

UNIT TESTS

Test 1
"The Tell-Tale Heart"

___ 1. Why did the narrator murder the old man?
    a. The old man had insulted him   b. The narrator had no reason
    c. The narrator did not like the old man's eye   d. The old man had insulted him

___ 2. What did the narrator repeatedly tell us?
    a. That he was not mad   b. That he was mad
    c. That the old man was mad   d. That he hated the old man

___ 3. What forced the old man to leap into the room?
    a. Someone pushed him   b. The old man was about to discover him
    c. Someone was coming   d. The beating of the heart

___ 4. How did the narrator actually kill the old man?
    a. He stabbed him   b. He suffocated him under the bed
    c. He strangled him   d. He bricked him up in a wall

___ 5. How did the narrator get rid of the corpse?
    a. He bricked it up in a wall   b. He buried it in the back yard
    c. He set fire to the house   d. He chopped it up and buried it under the floor

___ 6. Who came knocking at the door at 4 o'clock?
    a. The police   b. Some neighbors
    c. The old man's wife   d. No one; it was just a noise he imagined

___ 7. Why did the narrator confess murdering the old man?
    a. The police made him   b. He wanted a lighter jail sentence
    c. He heard a heartbeat   d. The body was discovered

___ 8. The most important element in the story is
    a. The murder of the old man   b. Showing the psychological state of the narrator
    c. The suspense   d. Showing the psychological state of the old man

___ 9. The climax of the story is when
    a. The narrator confesses   b. The narrator murders the old man
    c. The body is discovered   d. The narrator first hears the heartbeat

___ 10. What kind of story is "The Tell-Tale Heart?"
    a. Detective   b. Horror
    c. Gothic   d. Psychological

Test 1
"The Black Cat"

___ 1. Who was Pluto?
    a. The narrator   b. The narrator's dog
    c. The narrator's cat   c. All of the above

___ 2. What "disease" did the narrator have?
    a. He was an alcoholic   b. He used drugs
    c. He was melancholy   d. He had an inferiority complex

___ 3. What was the first violent action he took against the cat?
    a. He beat it senseless   b. He hit it with an axe
    c. He kicked it down the stairs   d. He cut out its eye

___ 4. What was the second violent action he took against the cat?
    a. He hanged it   b. He hit it with an axe
    c. He cut out its eye   d. He beat it senseless

___ 5. What happened to the narrator's home?
    a. It cracked and fell in   b. It disappeared
    c. It burned down   d. Nothing; he just dreamed something did

___ 6. What peculiar mark did the second cat have?
    a. One eye was missing   b. a & d
    c. It had rope marks around its neck   d. It had white "gallows" on its breast

___ 7. How did the narrator kill his wife?
    a. Hanged her   b. Pushed her down the stairs
    c. Bricked her up in a false wall   d. Hit her with an axe

___ 8. What did he do with her body?
    a. Bricked her up in a false wall   b. Chopped it up & buried it under the floor
    c. Buried it in the back yard   d. Put her in a vault

___ 9. How was the body discovered?
    a. It escaped from the vault   b. The cat screamed
    c. The narrator confessed   d. The police heard a heartbeat

___ 10. What type of story is "The Black Cat?"
    a. Psychological   b. Horror
    c. Gothic   d. Detective

Test 1
"The Fall of the House of Usher"

___ 1. Why was the narrator going to see Roderick Usher?
    a. Usher asked him to come   b. He just happened to be going by the house
    c. Madeline was ill   d. He was a doctor

___ 2. What was the diagnosis of Lady Madeline's disease?
    a. Alcoholism   b. Melancholy
    c. Insanity   d. Apathy & a wasting away of the person

___ 3. What did Usher want to do with his twin sister's body?
    a. Brick it up in a wall   b. Bury it
    c. Stick it in a vault   d. Burn it

___ 4. What happened as the narrator read the story to Usher?
    a. Madeline escaped   b. Usher fell asleep
    c. The house fell in   d. The narrator became paranoid

___ 5. What did the corpse of Lady Madeline do when it came into the narrator's room?
    a. Smiled an evil smile   b. Fell on Usher
    c. Stood in the doorway then left   d. Tried to kill the narrator

___ 6. What did the narrator do after Madeline came in?
    a. Fled   b. Coaxed her to the catacombs
    c. Tried to axe her   d. Found a hiding place

___ 7. What happened to Usher's house at the end of the story?
    a. It burned down   b. It became a grotesque old mansion
    c. Nothing; it was imaginary   d. It cracked and fell into the tarn

___ 8. What kind of a story is "The Fall of the House of Usher?"
    a. Horror   b. Detective
    c. Gothic   d. None of the above

Test 1 "The Murders in the Rue Morgue"

___ 1. Who is Dupin?
    a. The narrator
    b. A policeman
    c. The culprit
    d. A man who likes to solve mysteries

___ 2. Dupin says, "He is a very little fellow, that's true, and would do better for the Theatre des Varieties." What do we learn about Dupin from his making this statement?
    a. He likes the theater
    b. He has a keen eye for detail & analytical mind
    c. He is critical of others
    d. Nothing

___ 3. What newspaper article drew the attention of Dupin?
    a. One about Ourang-Outangs
    b. One about sailors
    c. One about Madame L'Espanaye
    d. One about rare books

___ 4. Where did the police find Madame L'Espanaye?
    a. Behind a brick wall
    b. Stuffed up the chimney
    c. Thrown out the window
    d. Strangled in her bed

___ 5. The voice of the second person the witnesses heard was
    a. A Frenchman
    b. A sailor
    c. A Spaniard
    d. None of the above

___ 6. Why did Dupin get involved with the murder case?
    a. He was just nosy
    b. The police hired him as a detective
    c. He was a friend of the accused
    d. The narrator insisted

___ 7. What did Dupin find that the police missed?
    a. Hair in Madame's hand
    b. A window that only appeared to be nailed closed
    c. A ribbon
    d. All of the above

___ 8. How did Dupin test his theory?
    a. Reenacted the crime
    b. Put an ad in the paper
    c. Confronted the police
    d. Employed the narrator

___ 9. What reward did Dupin want?
    a. The gold
    b. Information about the murders
    c. The Ourang-Outang
    d. None

___ 10. What was the reaction of the Prefect of Police to the solving of the murder?
    a. Delight
    b. Indifference
    c. Chagrin
    d. Sadness

___ 11. Where is the climax of the story?
    a. When the murders are done
    b. Finding the Ourang-Outang
    c. When Dupin confronts the sailor
    d. When the Prefect of Police hears the case is solved

Test 1
"The Purloined Letter"

___ 1. Who was Monsieur G---?
    a. He stole the letter   b. The Prefect of Police
    c. The narrator   d. The murderer

___ 2. Who was D---?
    a. He stole the letter   b. The Prefect of Police
    c. The narrator   d. The murderer

___ 3. What did Dupin give the Prefect of Police?
    a. The letter   b. 50,000 francs
    c. Nothing   d. Information leading to the thief

___ 4. Why did Dupin wear dark glasses?
    a. He was sensitive to light   b. He was blind
    c. They were a disguise   d. He didn't want D--- to see his eyes

___ 5. Why did Dupin leave a snuff box behind?
    a. It was a mistake   b. He wanted an excuse to return
    c. It belonged to D--   d. It contained a microphone

___ 6. Why did Dupin replace the letter with a facsimile?
    a. D-- might have noticed the theft   b. He wanted to cause the ruin of D--
    c. He wanted to get safely away   d. All of the above

___ 7. Dupin knew D-- as
    a. A mathematician   b. A poet
    c. A mathematician & a poet   d. An honorable man

___ 8. What kind of a story is "The Purloined Letter?"
    a. Detective   b. Gothic
    c. Double personality   d. Psychological

Test 1
"The Pit and the Pendulum"

___ 1. What is the first scene the narrator describes?
   a. The murder
   b. The courtroom
   c. The dungeon
   d. The basement

___ 2. After "swooning" and describing various states of being conscious, where does the narrator come to his senses?
   a. In a dungeon
   b. The courtroom
   c. On a table
   d. In a pit

___ 3. How did the narrator discover the pit?
   a. He woke up in it
   b. He fell into it
   c. He fell next to it
   d. He heard a rat fall into it

___ 4. What was hanging over the table?
   a. A razor-sharp crescent
   b. A clock pendulum
   b. A huge weight
   c. A bright light

___ 5. How did the narrator get free from the table?
   a. The knife cut the ropes
   b. He wriggled free
   c. His captors let him out
   d. Rats ate the ropes

___ 6. What was unusual about the walls of the narrator's room?
   a. They were very smooth
   b. They were irregular in shape
   c. They were bloody
   d. They moved

___ 7. What forces the narrator towards the pit?
   a. The walls
   b. The rats
   c. The pendulum
   d. Nothing; he was drugged & fell in

___ 8. What is the surprise ending?
   a. The pendulum stops
   b. The walls stop
   c. The pit was an illusion
   d. The narrator was only dreaming

___ 9. Where is the climax of the story?
   a. When the narrator is freed
   b. When the pendulum stops
   c. When the narrator wakes up
   d. When he wriggled free from the ropes

___ 10. What kind of story is "The Pit and the Pendulum?"
   a. Gothic
   b. Horror
   c. Psychological
   d. All of the above

Test 1
"The Masque of Red Death"

___ 1. What was the Red Death?
    a. A highly contagious disease   b. An evil spirit
    c. Prospero's split personality   d. An omen

___ 2. What was unusual about the rooms where the ball was held?
    a. They were all dark   b. They were each different colors
    c. They were grotesquely decorated   d. They each had bizarre-sounding clocks

___ 3. For what did the orchestra pause each hour?
    a. Prince Prospero to speak   b. The guests to drink a toast
    c. The clock to sound   d. A grotesque figure which appeared

___ 4. Why did the newly-arrived figure draw attention?
    a. He was dressed all in white   b. He was dressed as red death
    c. He was dressed as Prospero   c. His costume was empty

___ 5. Who unmasked the figure?
    a. No one   b. Prince Prospero
    c. The narrator   d. One of the guests

___ 6. Who or what was the figure?
    a. Red death   b. Prince Prospero
    c. Nothing; the guests imagined it   d. Nothing; Prince Prospero was dreaming

___ 7. Where is the climax?
    a. When the figure enters   b. When the clock strikes
    c. When the figure's identity is made known   d. When the rooms fall in

___ 8. What kind of story is "The Masque of Red Death?"
    a. Horror   b. Detective
    c. Gothic   d. Psychological

Test 1
"The Cask of Amontillado"

___ 1. Identify Amontillado.
    a. The narrator   b. A small animal
    c. A kind of wine   d. A disease caused by nitre

___ 2. Identify Montresor.
    a. The narrator   b. A connoisseur of wine
    c. A religious man   d. A French wine

___ 3. What does the narrator want Fortunato to do?
    a. Come see his catacombs   b. Taste some wine
    c. Join the Masons   d. Go with him to the carnival

___ 4. What does the narrator offer Fortunato as they walk along?
    a. Wine   b. Medicine
    c. Gold   d. Information about the Masons

___ 5. What "sign" did the narrator give Fortunato?
    a. A wink   b. A password
    c. A trowel   d. He rang some bells

___ 6. What happened to Fortunato?
    a. He got drunk   b. He was chained to a wall
    c. He was bricked in   d. All of the above

___ 7. Why didn't Fortunato resist?
    a. He was dumbfounded   b. He was having a good time
    c. He was drunk   d. a & c

___ 8. Why did the narrator's heart grow sick?
    a. He killed Fortunato   b. The dampness of the catacombs
    c. He had been cheated   d. The wine was no good

___ 9. What had Fortunato done to the narrator?
    a. Cheated him in a wine deal   b. Sent Luchesi to rob him
    c. Insulted him   d. a & b

___ 10. Who discovered the body?
    a. Luchesi   b. The police
    c. Dupin   d. No one

Test 1
Poe's Poems

From which poems are the lines below?

A. Annabel Lee   B. The Raven   C. To Helen   D. The Bells   E. Ulalume   F. Lenore

___ 1. "Only this and nothing more."

___ 2. "In a kingdom by the sea"

___ 3. "Fell on the upturn'd faces of the roses"

___ 4. "The leaves they were crisped and sere --"

___ 5. "What a world of merriment their melody foretells!"

___ 6. "Nevermore!"

___ 7. "This ghoul-haunted woodland of Weir"

___ 8. "And so, all the night-tide, I lie down by the side
Of my darling -- my darling -- my life and my bride,"

___ 9. "Come! let the burial rite be read -- the funeral song be sung! --
An anthem for the queenliest dead that ever died so young --"

___ 10. "Perched upon a bust of Pallas just above my chamber door --"

Test 2
"The Tell-Tale Heart"

___ 1. Why did the narrator murder the old man?
    a. The old man had insulted him   b. The narrator did not like the old man's eye
    c. The narrator had no reason   c. The old man had insulted him

___ 2. What did the narrator repeatedly tell us?
    a. That the old man was mad   b. That he was mad
    c. That he was not mad   d. That he hated the old man

___ 3. What forced the old man to leap into the room?
    a. The beating of the heart   b. The old man was about to discover him
    c. Someone was coming   d. Someone had pushed him

___ 4. How did the narrator actually kill the old man?
    a. He stabbed him   b. He bricked him up in a wall
    c. He strangled him   d. He suffocated him under the bed

___ 5. How did the narrator get rid of the corpse?
    a. He bricked it up in a wall   b. He buried it in the back yard
    c. He chopped it up and buried it under the floor   d. He set fire to the house

___ 6. Who came knocking at the door at 4 o'clock?
    a. Some neighbors   b. The police
    c. The old man's wife   d. No one; it was just a noise he imagined

___ 7. Why did the narrator confess murdering the old man?
    a. The police made him   b. He wanted a lighter jail sentence
    c. The body was discovered   d. He heard a heartbeat

___ 8. The most important element in the story is
    a. Showing the psychological state of the narrator   b. The suspense
    c. The murder of the old man   d. Showing the psychological state of the old man

___ 9. The climax of the story is when
    a. The narrator murders the old man   b. The narrator confesses
    c. The body is discovered   d. The narrator first hears the heartbeat

___10. What kind of story is "The Tell-Tale Heart?"
    a. Detective   b. Psychological
    c. Gothic   d. Horror

Test 2
"The Black Cat"

___ 1. Who was Pluto?
    a. The narrator   b. The narrator's cat
    c. The narrator's dog   c. All of the above

___ 2. What "disease" did the narrator have?
    a. He had an inferiority complex   b. He used drugs
    c. He was an alcoholic   d. He was melancholy

___ 3. What was the first violent action he took against the cat?
    a. He cut out its eye   b. He hit it with an axe
    c. He kicked it down the stairs   d. He beat it senseless

___ 4. What was the second violent action he took against the cat?
    a. He hit it with an axe   b. He hanged it
    c. He cut out its eye   d. He beat it senseless

___ 5. What happened to the narrator's home?
    a. It cracked and fell in   b. It disappeared
    c. It burned down   d. Nothing; he just dreamed something did

___ 6. What peculiar mark did the second cat have?
    a. One eye was missing   b. a & c
    c. It had white "gallows" on its breast d. It had rope marks around its neck

___ 7. How did the narrator kill his wife?
    a. Hanged her   b. Pushed her down the stairs
    c. Hit her with an axe   d. Bricked her up in a false wall

___ 8. What did he do with her body?
    a. Put her in a vault   b. Chopped it up & buried it under the floor
    c. Buried it in the back yard   d. Bricked her up in a false wall

___ 9. How was the body discovered?
    a. It escaped from the vault   b. The police heard a heartbeat
    c. The narrator confessed   d. The cat screamed

___ 10. What type of story is "The Black Cat?"
    a. Gothic   b. Horror
    c. Psychological   d. Detective

Test 2
"The Fall of the House of Usher"

___ 1. Why was the narrator going to see Roderick Usher?
    a. Madeline was ill   b. He just happened to be going by the house
    c. Usher asked him to come   d. He was a doctor

___ 2. What was the diagnosis of Lady Madeline's disease?
    a. Apathy & a wasting away of the person   b. Melancholy
    c. Insanity   d. Alcoholism

___ 3. What did Usher want to do with his twin sister's body?
    a. Brick it up in a wall   b. Bury it
    c. Burn it   d. Stick it in a vault

___ 4. What happened as the narrator read the story to Usher?
    a. Usher fell asleep   b. Madeline escaped
    c. The house fell in   d. The narrator became paranoid

___ 5. What did the corpse of Lady Madeline do when it came into the narrator's room?
    a. Fell on Usher   b. Smiled an evil smile
    c. Stood in the doorway then left   d. Tried to kill the narrator

___ 6. What did the narrator do after Madeline came in?
    a. Tried to axe her   b. Coaxed her to the catacombs
    c. Fled   d. Found a hiding place

___ 7. What happened to Usher's house at the end of the story?
    a. It burned down   b. It cracked and fell into the tarn
    c. Nothing; it was imaginary   d. It became a grotesque old mansion

___ 8. What kind of a story is "The Fall of the House of Usher?"
    a. Horror   b. Gothic
    c. Detective   d. None of the above

Test 2 "The Murders in the Rue Morgue"

___ 1. Who is Dupin?
    a. The narrator
    b. A man who likes to solve mysteries
    c. The culprit
    d. A policeman

___ 2. Dupin says, "He is a very little fellow, that's true, and would do better for the Theatre des Varieties." What do we learn about Dupin from his making this statement?
    a. He likes the theater
    b. Nothing
    c. He is critical of others
    d. He has a keen eye for detail & an analytical mind

___ 3. What newspaper article drew the attention of Dupin?
    a. One about Madame L'Espanaye
    b. One about sailors
    c. One about Ourang-Outangs
    d. One about rare books

___ 4. Where did the police find Madame L'Espanaye?
    a. Behind a brick wall
    b. Thrown out the window
    c. Stuffed up the chimney
    d. Strangled in her bed

___ 5. The voice of the second person the witnesses heard was
    a. A Frenchman
    b. A sailor
    c. A Spaniard
    d. None of the above

___ 6. Why did Dupin get involved with the murder case?
    a. He was just nosy
    b. He was a friend of the accused
    c. The police hired him as a detective
    d. The narrator insisted

___ 7. What did Dupin find that the police missed?
    a. Hair in Madame's hand
    b. A window that only appeared to be nailed closed
    c. A ribbon
    d. All of the above

___ 8. How did Dupin test his theory?
    a. Put an ad in the paper
    b. Reenacted the crime
    c. Confronted the police
    d. Employed the narrator

___ 9. What reward did Dupin want?
    a. The gold
    b. The Ourang-Outang
    c. Information about the murders
    d. None

___ 10. What was the reaction of the Prefect of Police to the solving of the murder?
    a. Delight
    b. Chagrin
    c. Indifference
    d. Sadness

___ 11. Where is the climax of the story?
    a. when the murders are done
    b. finding the Ourang-Outang
    c. when the Prefect of Police hears the case is solved
    d. when Dupin confronts the sailor

Test 2
"The Purloined Letter"

___ 1. Who was Monsieur G---?
    a. The Prefect of Police   b. He stole the letter
    c. The narrator   d. The murderer

___ 2. Who was D---?
    a. The murderer   b. The Prefect of Police
    c. The narrator   d. He stole the letter

___ 3. What did Dupin give the Prefect of Police?
    a. Nothing   b. 50,000 francs
    c. The letter   d. Information leading to the thief

___ 4. Why did Dupin wear dark glasses?
    a. He was sensitive to light   b. He was blind
    c. He didn't want D--- to see his eyes   d. They were a disguise

___ 5. Why did Dupin leave a snuff box behind?
    a. It was a mistake   b. It belonged to D--
    c. He wanted an excuse to return   d. It contained a microphone

___ 6. Why did Dupin replace the letter with a facsimile?
    a. D-- might have noticed the theft   b. He wanted to cause the ruin of D--
    c. He wanted to get safely away   d. All of the above

___ 7. Dupin knew D-- as
    a. A mathematician   b. A poet
    c. A mathematician & a poet   d. An honorable man

___ 8. What kind of a story is "The Purloined Letter?"
    a. Gothic   b. Detective
    c. Double personality   d. Psychological

Test 2
"The Pit and the Pendulum"

___ 1. What is the first scene the narrator describes?
    a. The murder
    b. The basement
    c. The dungeon
    d. The courtroom

___ 2. After "swooning" and describing various states of being conscious, where does the narrator come to his senses?
    a. The courtroom
    b. A dungeon
    c. On a table
    d. In a pit

___ 3. How did the narrator discover the pit?
    a. He fell next to it
    b. He fell into it
    c. He woke up in it
    d. He heard a rat fall into it

___ 4. What was hanging over the table?
    a. A huge weight
    b. A clock pendulum
    b. A razor-sharp crescent
    c. A bright light

___ 5. How did the narrator get free from the table?
    a. The knife cut the ropes
    b. He wriggled free
    c. Rats ate the ropes
    d. His captors let him out

___ 6. What was unusual about the walls of the narrator's room?
    a. They moved
    b. They were irregular in shape
    c. They were bloody
    d. They were very smooth

___ 7. What forces the narrator towards the pit?
    a. The pendulum
    b. The rats
    c. The walls
    d. Nothing; he was drugged & fell in

___ 8. What is the surprise ending?
    a. The pendulum stops
    b. The narrator was only dreaming
    c. The pit was an illusion
    d. The walls stop

___ 9. Where is the climax of the story?
    a. When the pendulum stops
    b. When the narrator is freed
    c. When the narrator wakes up
    d. When he wriggled free from the ropes

___ 10. What kind of story is "The Pit and the Pendulum?"
    a. Gothic
    b. Horror
    c. Psychological
    d. All of the above

Test 2
"The Masque of Red Death"

___ 1. What was the Red Death?
    a. An omen
    b. An evil spirit
    c. Prospero's split personality
    d. A highly contagious disease

___ 2. What was unusual about the rooms where the ball was held?
    a. They were each different colors
    b. They were all dark
    c. They were grotesquely decorated
    d. They each had bizarre-sounding clocks

___ 3. For what did the orchestra pause each hour?
    a. Prince Prospero to speak
    b. The clock to sound
    c. The guests to drink a toast
    d. A grotesque figure which appeared

___ 4. Why did the newly-arrived figure draw attention?
    a. He was dressed as red death
    b. He was dressed all in white
    c. He was dressed as Prospero
    d. His costume was empty

___ 5. Who unmasked the figure?
    a. The narrator
    b. Prince Prospero
    c. No one
    d. One of the guests

___ 6. Who or what was the figure?
    a. Nothing; Prince Prospero was dreaming
    b. Prince Prospero
    c. Nothing; the guests imagined it
    d. Red death

___ 7. Where is the climax?
    a. When the figure enters
    b. When the figure's identity is made known
    c. When the clock strikes
    d. When the rooms fall in

___ 8. What kind of story is "The Masque of Red Death?"
    a. Gothic
    b. Detective
    c. Horror
    d. Psychological

Test 2
"The Cask of Amontillado"

___ 1. Identify Amontillado.
    a. The narrator　　　　　　　　b. A kind of wine
    c. A small animal　　　　　　　d. A disease caused by nitre

___ 2. Identify Montresor.
    a. A religious man　　　　　　　b. A connoisseur of wine
    c. The narrator　　　　　　　　d. A French wine

___ 3. What does the narrator want Fortunato to do?
    a. Come see his catacombs　　　b. Go with him to the carnival
    c. Join the Masons　　　　　　d. Taste some wine

___ 4. What does the narrator offer Fortunato as they walk along?
    a. Medicine　　　　　　　　　b. Wine
    c. Gold　　　　　　　　　　　d. Information about the Masons

___ 5. What "sign" did the narrator give Fortunato?
    a. A wink　　　　　　　　　　b. A password
    c. He rang some bells　　　　　d. A trowel

___ 6. What happened to Fortunato?
    a. He got drunk　　　　　　　　b. He was chained to a wall
    c. He was bricked in　　　　　　d. All of the above

___ 7. Why didn't Fortunato resist?
    a. He was dumbfounded　　　　b. He was drunk
    c. a & b　　　　　　　　　　　d. He was having a good time

___ 8. Why did the narrator's heart grow sick?
    a. The dampness of the catacombs　b. He killed Fortunato
    c. He had been cheated　　　　　d. The wine was no good

___ 9. What had Fortunato done to the narrator?
    a. Cheated him in a wine deal　　b. Insulted him
    c. Sent Luchesi to rob him　　　d. a & b

___ 10. Who discovered the body?
    a. Luchesi　　　　　　　　　　b. The police
    c. Dupin　　　　　　　　　　　d. No one

Test 2
Poe's Poems

From which poems are the lines below?

A. Lenore   B. Annabel Lee   C. The Raven   D. To Helen   E. The Bells   F. Ulalume

___ 1. "Only this and nothing more."

___ 2. "In a kingdom by the sea"

___ 3. "Fell on the upturn'd faces of the roses"

___ 4. "The leaves they were crisped and sere --"

___ 5. "What a world of merriment their melody foretells!"

___ 6. "Nevermore!"

___ 7. "This ghoul-haunted woodland of Weir"

___ 8. "And so, all the night-tide, I lie down by the side
Of my darling -- my darling -- my life and my bride,"

___ 9. "Come! let the burial rite be read -- the funeral song be sung! --
An anthem for the queenliest dead that ever died so young --"

___ 10. "Perched upon a bust of Pallas just above my chamber door --"

ESSAY QUESTIONS - EDGAR ALLAN POE UNIT

1. Choose two of Poe's narrators and compare and contrast them.

2. Choose any two of Poe's stories and explain and define the form in which they are written using specific examples for illustration.

3. Explain why Poe used the first person narrative. Include examples of how he used the narrators from at least three stories.

4. Poe believed strongly in writing for <u>effect</u>. Explain how he does so using examples from at least three different stories.

5. Poe was fascinated by the ease with which one could easily slip from the rational to the irrational. Explain how he uses this conflict using at least two different stories for examples.

6. Characterize Poe's writing style using at least four different stories for examples.

Vocabulary 1
Edgar Allan Poe Stories

Listen to the words and write them down next to the numbers.
Go back later and write down the definitions.

1.
2.
3.
4.
5.
6.
7.
8.
9.
10.
11.
12.
13.
14.
15.

Vocabulary 2
Edgar Allan Poe Stories

Listen to the vocabulary words and write them down. Go back later and write a composition using all of the words. The composition must in some way relate to the Poe stories unit.

Vocabulary 3
Edgar Allan Poe Stories

Match the correct definitions to the words.

____ 1. MANIFOLD   A. A ghostly figure

____ 2. APPARITION   B. One of many kinds

____ 3. DISSIMULATION   C. Manner

____ 4. SULTRINESS   D. Responsible; at fault

____ 5. IMPUNITY   E. Eyes

____ 6. SUBLIME   F. Can't be turned back

____ 7. LIVID   G. Shrewd

____ 8. MIEN   H. Exemption from punishment, penalty, or harm

____ 9. SAGACIOUS   I. Age; time

____ 10. PRODIGIOUS   J. To find out

____ 11. CONSIGNED   K. Concealing one's true feelings or intentions

____ 12. IRREVOCABLE   L. Majestic; inspiring awe; impressive

____ 13. ASCERTAIN   M. To strengthen or support with other evidence

____ 14. CULPABLE   N. Enormous

____ 15. EPOCH   O. Wise

____ 16. ORBS   P. Bruised

____ 17. COGNIZANT   Q. Handed over

____ 18. NEBULOUS   R. Aware; familiar with

____ 19. CORROBORATES   S. Cloudy, misty, or hazy

____ 20. ASTUTE   T. Sensualness; voluptuousness

Vocabulary 4
E. A. Poe Stories

Match the correct definitions to the words.

____ 1. EGRESS   A. A ghostly figure

____ 2. ORBS   B. Into separate parts or pieces

____ 3. COVETED   C. Boldness; daring

____ 4. IMPUNITY   D. Cloudy, misty, or hazy

____ 5. VEXED   E. One of many kinds

____ 6. ASCERTAIN   F. Exit; escape

____ 7. MIEN   G. Exemption from punishment, penalty, or harm

____ 8. ASUNDER   H. Casually; randomly

____ 9. APPARITION   I. The quality of being discerning, sound in judgment

____ 10. AUDACITY   J. Eyes

____ 11. NEBULOUS   K. Wished for longingly

____ 12. LIVID   L. To bring distress or suffering to; plague

____ 13. IRREVOCABLE   M. To find out

____ 14. SAGACITY   N. Pale; dull

____ 15. SAGACIOUS   O. Manner

____ 16. PALLID   P. Can't be turned back

____ 17. MANIFOLD   Q. Bruised

____ 18. CONSIGNED   R. Inspired; captivated

____ 19. ENAMORED   S. Wise

____ 20. PROMISCUOUSLY T. Handed over

ANSWER KEY VOCABULARY 3
E. A. Poe Stories

1. B
2. A
3. K
4. T
5. H
6. L
7. P
8. C
9. O
10. N
11. Q
12. F
13. J
14. D
15. I
16. E
17. R
18. S
19. M
20. G

ANSWER KEY VOCABULARY 4
E. A. Poe Stories

1. F
2. J
3. K
4. G
5. L
6. M
7. O
8. B
9. A
10. C
11. D
12. Q
13. P
14. I
15. S
16. N
17. E
18. T
19. R
20. H

ANSWER KEYS: Edgar Allan Poe Unit Test 1 Sections

<u>The Tell-Tale Heart</u>
1. C
2. A
3. D
4. B
5. D
6. A
7. C
8. B
9. A
10. D

<u>The Black Cat</u>
1. C
2. A
3. D
4. A
5. C
6. B
7. D
8. A
9. B
10. A

<u>Fall of the House of Usher</u>
1. A
2. D
3. C
4. A
5. B
6. A
7. D
8. C

<u>Murders in the Rue Morgue</u>
1. D
2. B
3. C
4. B
5. D
6. C
7. D
8. B
9. B
10. C
11. C

<u>The Purloined Letter</u>
1. B
2. A
3. A
4. D
5. B
6. D
7. C
8. A

<u>The Pit and the Pendulum</u>
1. B
2. A
3. C
4. A
5. D
6. D
7. A
8. B
9. A
10. D

<u>Masque of Red Death</u>
1. A
2. B
3. C
4. B
5. A
6. A
7. C
8. A

<u>Cask of Amontillado</u>
1. C
2. A
3. B
4. A
5. C
6. D
7. D
8. B
9. C
10. D

<u>Poetry</u>
1. B
2. A
3. C
4. E
5. D
6. B
7. E
8. A
9. F
10. B

ANSWER KEYS: Edgar Allan Poe Unit Test 2 Sections

<u>The Tell-Tale Heart</u>

1. B
2. C
3. A
4. D
5. C
6. B
7. D
8. A
9. B
10. B

<u>The Black Cat</u>

1. B
2. C
3. A
4. B
5. A
6. B
7. C
8. D
9. D
10. C

<u>Fall of the House of Usher</u>

1. C
2. A
3. D
4. B
5. A
6. C
7. B
8. B

<u>Murders in the Rue Morgue</u>

1. B
2. D
3. A
4. C
5. D
6. B
7. D
8. A
9. C
10. B
11. D

<u>The Purloined Letter</u>

1. A
2. D
3. C
4. C
5. C
6. D
7. C
8. B

<u>The Pit and the Pendulum</u>

1. D
2. B
3. A
4. B
5. C
6. A
7. C
8. D
9. B
10. B

<u>Masque of Red Death</u>

1. D
2. A
3. B
4. A
5. C
6. D
7. B
8. C

<u>Cask of Amontillado</u>

1. B
2. C
3. D
4. B
5. D
6. D
7. C
8. A
9. B
10. D

<u>Poetry</u>

1. C
2. B
3. D
4. F
5. E
6. C
7. F
8. B
9. A
10. C

UNIT RESOURCE MATERIALS

BULLETIN BOARD IDEAS - *Poe Stories*

1. Leave a portion of the bulletin board for the students' best writing assignments.

2. Write out some of the significant quotes from the text on colorful construction paper. Cut out letters to title the board *Poe Stories*.

3. Take one of the word search puzzles and draw it (enlarged) on the bulletin board. Write the clue words to find to one side. Invite students to take pens and find and circle the words in the time before and after class (or perhaps if they finish their work early).

4. Take snapshots of the students in their costumes (or have the newspaper or yearbook staff take them.) Post the pictures on the bulletin board. Keep the pictures from year to year and pretty soon you'll have a lot of material for a fun bulletin board!

5. Enlarge and post articles about *Poe Stories*.

6. Find pictures from cartoons, comic books or magazines to represent some of the different characters from Poe's stories. Put them up on the board. Draw comic strip bubbles from them and write in various characterizing quotes. (For example, find a bizarre-looking character and have him say, "True! -- nervous -- very, very dreadfully nervous I had been and am; but why will you say that I am mad?")

7. Make a bulletin board about Poe and his works. Write a biography of Poe in the center of the board. Make cut-out "books," one for each of the works covered in this unit. Put the title on each "book" and inside write a little summary of the plot.

8. Title the board EDGAR ALLAN POE: A MASTER OF LITERARY FORM. Divide the board into six sections, one for each form of story Poe used: Detective Stories, Stories of Psychology, Stories of Double Personality, Horror Stories, Gothic Stories, and Poetry. Inside each section, write a brief description of the major characteristics of that type of form. Make a little "book" of each of Poe's stories and post them in the appropriate sections on the board.

EXTRA ACTIVITIES

One of the difficulties in teaching literature is that all students don't read at the same speed. One student who likes to read may take the book home and finish it in a day or two. Sometimes a few students finish the in-class assignments early. The problem, then, is finding suitable extra activities for students.

The best thing I've found is to keep a little library in the classroom. For this unit on *Poe Stories,* you might check out from the school library other related books and articles about castles, history of the period, pilgrimages, the occupations mentioned in the text, or the history of the Church in England. Also, you might include other works by Poe (either in original text or simplified versions) and articles of criticism about *Poe Stories*.

Other things you may keep on hand are puzzles. We have made some relating directly to *Poe Stories* for you. Feel free to duplicate them.

Some students may like to draw. You might devise a contest or allow some extra-credit grade for students who draw characters or scenes from *Poe Stories*. Note, too, that if the students do not want to keep their drawings you may pick up some extra bulletin board materials this way. If you have a contest and you supply the prize (a record album or something like that perhaps), you could, possibly, make the drawing itself a non-refundable entry fee.

The pages which follow contain games, puzzles and worksheets. The keys, when appropriate, immediately follow the puzzle or worksheet. There are two main groups of activities: one group for the unit; that is, generally relating to *Poe Stories* text, and another group of activities related strictly to *Poe Stories* vocabulary.

Directions for these games, puzzles and worksheets are self-explanatory. The object here is to provide you with extra materials you may use in any way you choose.

MORE ACTIVITIES - *Poe Stories*

1. Have students design a book cover for Poe's stories.

2. Have students design a bulletin board (ready to be put up; not just sketched) for Poe's stories.

3. Use some of the related topics (noted earlier for an in-class library) as topics for research, reports or written papers, or as topics for guest speakers.

4. Have a psychologist come in and psychoanalyze a few of Poe's characters.

5. Have students write a story imitating one of the types of stories used in Poe's stories (for example, a detective or horror story).

6. Research what careers are currently available for someone interested in writing fiction or poetry.

7. Have students write a description of an event that has recently taken place using Poe's writing style.

8. Have students read Poe's "Philosophy of Composition."

9. Have students think of other examples of books, TV shows, or movies which show the influence of Poe's philosophies of composition.

WORD SEARCH - Poe Stories

```
M Z Z G K B E H K Y N V F V K B D P F F S S Z R
Y M D Y N A D S B O G Q Q M E S C O O L L F O K
N F T E K E X E U H R M R L R Y A H O L O L O N
N I W T R A V E N O B E L I M I S C A F I O G K
P V P A S E Y E T I H S P E J A A W H A B C R N
S V T U M E V U R S O L R S B T S H S I H N E G
T S A L D E L E U M L L ' O P A C Q C Y M X G G
M R G U S P G Z N D O E R E P O N R U E D N C M
P A O P L U D A E G V R T U S E R N E E B I E Y
H J D W T T F T L I E D E T P P Q P A C H O O Y
M B M P E H A F T L F X U Z E Q A T C T E D N G
S O F V E L B C O L O M H N D R H N O K A S P Y
H Y N A I N E X J C E W A X G G B G A L X R S K
P M R T J D D Z L S A T S D C E K K L Y M D C R
S T U T R K D U J C R T R C E J O I P B E I P B
J M D R X E C L L T H Y E G Y L T N Z L R B S Z
S V N Y X H S P X U L N W D T N I K X E T K L F
Q S W K E P D O Z C M D B P O M B N D W P L Q Y
R Y L S S R H Q R N F J B M K V B O E T Y P X G
L L I D E T E C T I V E A Z T S R H S V R Z P M
```

AMONTILLADO	EBONY	MADELINE	RED
ANNABEL	EYE	MASQUE	REVENGE
AXE	FACSIMILE	MONTRESOR	RODERICK
BELLS	FLOOR	MUTILATED	ROPE
BOOK	FOOD	NEVERMORE	SAILOR
CASK	GALLOWS	PENDULUM	SEVEN
CAT	GOTHIC	PIT	SUFFOCATED
CHAIR	HEART	PLUTO	TROWEL
CHIMNEY	HOUSE	POLICE	TWIN
COSTUMES	L'ESPANAYE	PROPSPERO	USHER
DEATH	LE BON	PURLOINED	VAULT
DETECTIVE	LETTER	RATS	WALLS
DUNGEON	LUCHESI	RAVEN	
DUPIN	MAD	RECESS	

CROSSWORD - *Poe Stories*

CROSSWORD CLUES - Edgar Allan Poe Stories

ACROSS
1. Murderer placed his --- over the place where he put the corpse (TTH)
3. --- of Amontillado (CA)
6. Red ---; a highly contagious disease (MRD)
7. Crazy (TTH)
8. Narrator's --- burned down, leaving figure of a cat and rope on one wall (BC)
11. Vulture (TTH)
12. Sign of a mason (CA)
13. Madame --- and Mademoiselle Camille ---- (RM)
14. Murder ___ the Rue Morgue
15. Create
16. Narrator murdered his wife with one (BC)
17. The --- and the Pendulum (PP)
18. Holds blood in the body; pathway for blood
19. Masque of --- Death (MRD)
21. Number of rooms in use at the Prince's ball (MRD)
25. The murderer put the corpse under the --- boards (TTH)
27. Cask of --- (CA)
30. Holes in skin where sweat comes out
31. Very warm
33. Tell an untruth
34. Opposite of lose
35. Unhappy
36. Opposite of less
38. Narrator thought white on the second cat's breast looked like --- (BC)
42. The Pit and the --- (PP)
45. Montresor said he could taste the wine if Fortunato were busy (CA)
46. Definite article
47. Narrator hanged his cat with one (BC)
48. Prefix 'un' means ---
49. Brief time of rest or relief
50. Fall of the House of --- (FHU)
51. Negative reply
52. Lady ---- (FHU)

DOWN
1. What people wore to the ball (MRD)
2. The Black --- (BC)
3. Place narrator disposed of his wife's body (BC)
4. The ourang-outang belonged to him
5. To the ryhming and chiming of the ---
6. Come to a conclusion by reasoning
7. --- of Red Death (MRD)
8. The Tell-Tale ---- (TTH)
9. Color of clock (MRD)
10. Narrator met Dupin looking for the same rare --- (RM)
16. --- Lee; she lived in a kingdom by the sea
20. Kind of story with mansion, dark tombs beneath/inside; ominous setting, living corpse (FHU)
22. Place where Usher put his twin sister's body (FHU)
23. Quoth the Raven '----'
24. Dupin replaced the letter with a — (PL)
25. Narrator put this on the ropes (PP)
26. Narrator wanted them to eat the ropes (PP)
28. Usher put his --- sister'sbody in a vault (FHU)
29. Person accused of murders in Rue St. Morgue (RM)
30. The Prince (MRD)
32. Setting for the story (PP)
37. Montresor bricked Fortunato into a --- in the wall (CA)
39. It was stolen (PL)
40. The cat's name (BC)
41. Montresor's motive (CA)
43. The detective (RM)
44. Murderer greeted them warmly (TTH)

CROSSWORD ANSWER KEY - *Poe Stories*

	C	H	A	I	R				C		C	A	S	K								
	O					B		D	E	A	T	H		A		M	A	D	H	O	U	S	E
	S		B			E	Y	E		T		I		I		A			E				B
	T	R	O	W	E	L		D				M		L	E	S	P	A	N	A	Y	E	O
	U		O			L	O	U	D			N		O		Q			R				N
	M	A	K	E	S			C		A	X	E		R		U		P	I	T			Y
	E					V	E	I	N		Y			R	E	D				G			
	S	E	V	E	N			N								F		F	L	O	O	R	
			A		E				A	M	O	N	T	I	L	L	A	D	O		T		A
			U		V		P		B			W		E		C		O		H	O	T	
D		L	I	E		R	A	V	E	N		I		B		S	A	D		I			S
U		T		R		O			L			N		O		I				C			
N				M		P						N		M	O	R	E						
G	A	L	L	O	W	S				P				I		E		R					
E		E		R		P	E	N	D	U	L	U	M		P		L	U	C	H	E	S	I
O		T	H	E		E				U		U		R	O	P	E		E		V		
N	O	T				R	E	S	P	I	T	E			L		U	S	H	E	R		
		E				O		I		O					I				S		N		
		R				N	O							C				G					
								M	A	D	E	L	I	N	E		E						

159

MATCHING QUIZ/WORKSHEET 1 - *Poe Stories*

____ 1. REVENGE   A. Crazy (TTH)

____ 2. RAVEN   B. Montresor bricked Fortunato into a --- in the wall (CA)

____ 3. RED   C. Fall of the House of --- (FHU)

____ 4. USHER   D. He decided to kill Fortunato (CA)

____ 5. RECESS   E. Murderer greeted them warmly (TTH)

____ 6. CAT   F. The Black --- (BC)

____ 7. AMONTILLADO   G. Narrator met Dupin looking for the same rare --- (RM)

____ 8. RATS   H. Narrator wanted them to eat the ropes (PP)

____ 9. SEVEN   I. What people wore to the ball (MRD)

____ 10. BOOK   J. The Prince (MRD)

____ 11. MAD   K. Quoth the --- 'Nevermore'

____ 12. FLOOR   L. The murderer put the corpse under the --- boards (TTH)

____ 13. TWIN   M. Narrator murdered his wife with one (BC)

____ 14. PROPSPERO   N. Masque of --- Death (MRD)

____ 15. POLICE   O. Number of rooms in use at the Prince's ball (MRD)

____ 16. BELLS   P. The ourang-outang belonged to him (RM)

____ 17. AXE   Q. Montresor's motive (CA)

____ 18. MONTRESOR   R. Cask of --- (CA)

____ 19. SAILOR   S. Usher put his --- sister's body in a vault (FHU)

____ 20. COSTUMES   T. To the rhyming and chiming of the ---

MATCHING QUIZ/WORKSHEET 2 - *Poe Stories*

____ 1. PENDULUM   A. Usher put his --- sister's body in a vault (FHU)

____ 2. WALLS   B. It was stolen (PL)

____ 3. GOTHIC   C. To the rhyming and chiming of the ---

____ 4. BELLS   D. Quoth the Raven '----'

____ 5. DEATH   E. --- of Red Death (MRD)

____ 6. EYE   F. Kind of story with mansion, dark tombs beneath/inside; ominous setting, living corpse (FHU)

____ 7. RATS   G. Red ---; a highly contagious disease (MRD)

____ 8. NEVERMORE   H. Sign of a mason (CA)

____ 9. ANNABEL   I. They moved inward (PP)

____ 10. PIT   J. Vulture (TTH)

____ 11. EBONY   K. Narrator met Dupin looking for the same rare --- (RM)

____ 12. MASQUE   L. Montresor bricked Fortunato into a --- in the wall (CA)

____ 13. TROWEL   M. --- Lee; she lived in a kingdom by the sea

____ 14. BOOK   N. The --- and the Pendulum (PP)

____ 15. TWIN   O. Number of rooms in use at the Prince's ball (MRD)

____ 16. SEVEN   P. The Pit and the --- (PP)

____ 17. RECESS   Q. Narrator wanted them to eat the ropes (PP)

____ 18. LETTER   R. Condition of Madame L'Espanaye's corpse (RM)

____ 19. GALLOWS   S. Narrator thought white on the second cat's breast looked like --- (BC)

____ 20. MUTILATED   T. Color of clock (MRD)

KEY: MATCHING QUIZ/WORKSHEETS - *Poe Stories*

Worksheet 1	Worksheet 2
1. Q	1. P
2. K	2. I
3. N	3. F
4. C	4. C
5. B	5. G
6. F	6. J
7. R	7. Q
8. H	8. D
9. O	9. M
10. G	10. N
11. A	11. T
12. L	12. E
13. S	13. H
14. J	14. K
15. E	15. A
16. T	16. O
17. M	17. L
18. D	18. B
19. P	19. S
20. I	20. R

JUGGLE LETTER REVIEW GAME CLUE SHEET - *Poe Stories*

SCRAMBLED	WORD	CLUE
LITDAONAMOL	AMONTILLADO	Cask of --- (CA)
NEBAALN	ANNABEL	--- Lee; she lived in a kingdom by the sea
EAX	AXE	Narrator murdered his wife with one (BC)
SLEBL	BELLS	To the rhyming and chiming of the ---
OKOB	BOOK	Narrator met Dupin looking for the same rare ---
SACK	CASK	--- of Amontillado (CA)
ACT	CAT	The Black --- (BC)
RHACI	CHAIR	Murderer placed his --- over the place where he put the corpse
YNHEMIC	CHIMNEY	Place narrator disposed of his wife's body
SMTEUOSC	COSTUMES	What people wore to the ball (MRD)
ETAHD	DEATH	Red ---; a highly contagious disease (MRD)
EDITVEECT	DETECTIVE	Dupin was the ---- (RM)
NENOGDU	DUNGEON	Setting for the story (PP)
NIDPU	DUPIN	The detective (RM)
BEYNO	EBONY	Color of clock (MRD)
YEE	EYE	Vulture --- (TTH)
SCALEFIMI	FACSIMILE	Dupin replaced the letter with a --- (PL)
OLROF	FLOOR	The murderer put the corpse under the — boards
ODFO	FOOD	Narrator put this on the ropes (PP)
WALSLOG	GALLOWS	Narrator thought white on the second cat's breast looked like ---
TCHOGI	GOTHIC	Kind of story with mansion, dark tombs beneath/inside; ominous setting, living corpse
RATEH	HEART	The Tell-Tale ---- (TTH)
SEUHO	HOUSE	Narrator's --- burned down, leaving figure of a cat and rope on one wall (BC)
NALSEPYEA	L'ESPANAYE	Madame --- and Mademoiselle Camille ---- (RM)
OLENB	LE BON	Person accused of murders in Rue St. Morgue (RM)
TRELET	LETTER	It was stolen (PL)
HIUCESL	LUCHESI	Montresor said he could taste the wine if Fortunato were busy
ADM	MAD	Crazy (TTH)

Poe Stories Juggle Letter Review Game Clues Continued

Scrambled	Answer	Clue
NAMDEEIL	MADELINE	Lady ---- (FHU)
UQSEMA	MASQUE	--- of Red Death (MRD)
RNORSOETM	MONTRESOR	He decided to kill Fortunato (CA)
LEDTUTIAM	MUTILATED	Condition of Madame L'Espanaye's corpse (RM)
VEOEMNRER	NEVERMORE	Quoth the Raven '----'
MUEPNULD	PENDULUM	The Pit and the --- (PP)
PTI	PIT	The --- and the Pendulum (PP)
LOTUP	PLUTO	The cat's name (BC)
ICLEOP	POLICE	Murderer greeted them warmly (TTH)
RPEOOPRS	PROSPERO	The Prince (MRD)
NDLOERUPI	PURLOINED	The --- Letter (PL)
RTAS	RATS	Narrator wanted them to eat the ropes (PP)
VANER	RAVEN	Quoth the --- 'Nevermore'
CEERSS	RECESS	Montresor bricked Fortunato into a --- in the wall
ERD	RED	Masque of --- Death (MRD)
EEEGVNR	REVENGE	Montresor's motive (CA)
DECRKORI	RODERICK	Mr. Usher (FHU)
PORE	ROPE	Narrator hanged his cat with one (BC)
LAROIS	SAILOR	The ourang-outang belonged to him (RM)
VEENS	SEVEN	Number of rooms in use at the Prince's ball
FATFOCDEUS	SUFFOCATED	How the old man died (TTH)
WROLET	TROWEL	Sign of a mason (CA)
WNIT	TWIN	Usher put his --- sister's body in a vault
SHURE	USHER	Fall of the House of --- (FHU)
LATUV	VAULT	Place where Usher put his twin sister's body
SLAWL	WALLS	They moved inward (PP)

VOCABULARY RESOURCE MATERIALS

VOCABULARY WORD SEARCH - *Poe Stories*

All words in this list are associated with *Poe Stories* with an emphasis on the vocabulary words chosen for study in the text. The words are placed backwards, forward, diagonally, up and down. The included words are listed below.

```
E N A M O R E D A P A L L I D A S T U T E R E S
G S I D M H E U T N B C M U P L P A N L E D H S
T E T L K D D Y V Q N P O P C S O A G Q I B Y S
N C G D E A D N S E U I A O S I Z F U A E V U Z
H Q D P C E J U D N X R H C R I D I I L C O I G
L C M I T Y O E I Z I E I I N O E E B N I I N D
Z I T E R I B T P T P T D G L M B A R G A I T J
D Y V S C M Y Y I Z A T O Q A A P O E I L M D Y
J O G A U B R O L T T C I L M L T R R I S I M J
C B G C K L N U S S K N E R U H G E U A S I P F
Y A C G G D T C N W U V Y C R E W G J S T R O Y
S U P Q Q T E R C P O O D Y N E E Z I L O E Q N
S Q X X Y R Z O I L E E U I T B V M V D Z P S Q
S Q K G Y Q N T E N N R A C E I U O I G P G P Y
X U Z L M C L N J G E T C M S L C G C C R E Q V
M P O T E Q C V I Y R S I E A I I A N A G P T Y
L P C I F E J S H E X L S T I O M D R R B Y B S
X S V J D Z N F C K B N I G U V Y O E O W L B W
N E B U L O U S Z U M O S S E N E S R E V R E P
D I M A C G A A S U N D E R V W S D E P O C H Y
```

AMID	COVETED	LIVID	REQUIEM
ANNIHILATE	CULPABLE	LUCID	SAGACIOUS
APPARITION	DERISION	MALEVOLENCE	SAGACITY
ASCERTAIN	DISSIMULATION	MANIFOLD	SERE
ASTUTE	ECSTATIC	MIEN	SUBLIME
ASUNDER	EGREGIOUS	NEBULOUS	SUCCUMBED
AUDACITY	EGRESS	ODIOUS	SULTRINESS
BEGUILING	ENAMORED	ORBS	UNPERCEIVED
COGNIZANT	EPOCH	PALLID	VEXED
CONCEIVED	IMPEDED	PERVERSENESS	VORACITY
CONSIGNED	IMPUNITY	PRODIGIOUS	
CORROBORATES	IRREVOCABLE	PROMISCUOUSLY	

VOCABULARY CROSSWORD - *Poe Stories*

VOCABULARY CROSSWORD CLUES - Poe Stories

ACROSS
1. Aware; familiar with
4. Deceiving; diverting
9. Responsible; at fault
11. Wished for longingly
12. Shrewd
14. To form or develop in the mind; devise
16. Boldness; daring
18. Related a story
19. A hymn, composition, or service for the dead
22. Narrator wanted them to eat the ropes (PP)
23. Withered; dry
25. A ghostly figure
27. To bring distress or suffering to; plague
28. Narrator met Dupin looking for the same rare --- (RM)
30. Evoking feelings of repulsion
32. Number of rooms in use at the Prince's ball (MRD)
33. Murder ___ the Rue Morgue
35. Concealing one's true feelings or intentions
37. Age; time
42. In the middle of
43. Usher put his --- sister's body in a vault (FHU)
45. Can't be turned back
46. Narrator murdered his wife with one (BC)
47. Narrator hanged his cat with one (BC)
48. Enormous

DOWN
2. Eyes
3. Cloudy, misty, or hazy
5. Vulture (TTH)
6. Bruised
7. The prefix 'un' means ---
8. One of many kinds
10. Easily understood; sane or rational
12. To find out
13. Euphoric; blissful
15. Bad or offensive
16. Into separate parts or pieces
17. Obstructed
20. Exit; escape
21. Scoffing; ridicule
24. Manner
26. To reduce to nonexistence; to nullify or render void; abolish
29. In equal amounts
31. Inspired; captivated
34. Majestic; inspiring awe; impressive
36. The ourang-outang belonged to him (RM)
38. Pale; dull
39. The Black --- (BC)
40. Murderer placed his --- over the place where he put the corpse (TTH)
41. The --- and the Pendulum (PP)
44. Crazy (TTH)

VOCABULARY CROSSWORD ANSWER KEY - *Poe Stories*

	C	O	G	N	I	Z	A	N	T			B	E	G	U	I	L	I	N	G		
		R		E					M		Y				I			O				
		B		B		C	U	L	P	A	B	L	E		C	O	V	E	T	E	D	
A	S	T	U	T	E				U		N				I							
S						C	O	N	C	E	I	V	E	D		A	U	D	A	C	I	T	Y
C				L		O			S		I		F		G		S					M	
E				U		T	O	L	D		O		R	E	Q	U	I	E	M		P		D
R	A	T	S			A					L		E		N		G		S	E	R	E	
T						T		M			D		G				D		R		D		R
A	P	P	A	R	I	T	I	O	N				I		V	E	X	E	D		E		I
I			N		C		E			B	O	O	K		R		S				D		S
N			N		C		N			U			E				S						O
	O	D	I	O	U	S				E		S	E	V	E	N		D	U	P	I	N
			H				S		N				E										
		D	I	S	S	I	M	U	L	A	T	I	O	N			E	P	O	C	H		
			L		A		B		M					C		A				A		P	
		A	M	I	D		L		O					H		L		T	W	I	N		
	M		T		L		I	R	R	E	V	O	C	A	B	L	E				T		
	A	X	E		O		M		E					I		I							
	D			R	O	P	E		D				P	R	O	D	I	G	I	O	U	S	

VOCABULARY WORKSHEET 1 - *Poe Stories*

___ 1. Exemption from punishment, penalty, or harm
    A. Requiem   B. Sere   C. Impunity   D. Sublime

___ 2. To form or develop in the mind; devise
    A. Pallid   B. Beguiling   C. Conceived   D. Irrevocable

___ 3. Bad or offensive
    A. Manifold   B. Corroborates   C. Consigned   D. Egregious

___ 4. To strengthen or support with other evidence
    A. Corroborates   B. Enamored   C. Cognizant   D. Amid

___ 5. Aware; familiar with
    A. Unperceived   B. Pallid   C. Sagacious   D. Cognizant

___ 6. Unnoticed
    A. Unperceived   B. Amid   C. Culpable   D. Orbs

___ 7. Into separate parts or pieces
    A. Asunder   B. Sagacious   C. Malevolence   D. Prodigious

___ 8. Cloudy, misty, or hazy
    A. Egregious   B. Sultriness   C. Nebulous   D. Sere

___ 9. Manner
    A. Mien   B. Epoch   C. Culpable   D. Conceived

___ 10. A hymn, composition, or service for the dead
    A. Egress   B. Consigned   C. Sagacious   D. Requiem

___ 11. Boldness; daring
    A. Audacity   B. Manifold   C. Lucid   D. Coveted

___ 12. Gave in
    A. Sultriness   B. Succumbed   C. Annihilate   D. Consigned

___ 13. A ghostly figure
    A. Astute   B. Apparition   C. Sagacity   D. Cognizant

___ 14. Majestic; inspiring awe; impressive
    A. Livid   B. Countenances   C. Sublime   D. Requiem

___ 15. Handed over
    A. Consigned   B. Coveted   C. Livid   D. Beguiling

___ 16. Evoking feelings of repulsion
    A. Ecstatic   B. Impunity   C. Epoch   D. Odious

___ 17. One of many kinds
    A. Egress   B. Dissimulation   C. Sagacious   D. Manifold

___ 18. Concealing one's true feelings or intentions
    A. Malevolence   B. Enamored   C. Dissimulation   D. Irrevocable

___ 19. Responsible; at fault
    A. Requiem   B. Epoch   C. Culpable   D. Audacity

___ 20. Sensualness; voluptuousness
    A. Promiscuously   B. Pallid   C. Sultriness   D. Amid

VOCABULARY WORKSHEET 2 - *Poe Stories*

____ 1. BEGUILING   A. Aware; familiar with

____ 2. COGNIZANT   B. Responsible; at fault

____ 3. LIVID   C. Boldness; daring

____ 4. ODIOUS   D. Sensualness; voluptuousness

____ 5. CULPABLE   E. Easily understood; sane or rational

____ 6. COVETED   F. Cloudy, misty, or hazy

____ 7. SERE   G. Inspired; captivated

____ 8. ANNIHILATE   H. Gave in

____ 9. AUDACITY   I. Bruised

____ 10. NEBULOUS   J. Handed over

____ 11. SUCCUMBED   K. Unnoticed

____ 12. CONSIGNED   L. Age; time

____ 13. SULTRINESS   M. To form or develop in the mind; devise

____ 14. UNPERCEIVED   N. Deceiving; diverting

____ 15. CONCEIVED   O. Majestic; inspiring awe; impressive

____ 16. SUBLIME   P. Wished for longingly

____ 17. ENAMORED   Q. To reduce to nonexistence; to nullify or render void; abolish

____ 18. EPOCH   R. Obstructed

____ 19. IMPEDED   S. Withered; dry

____ 20. LUCID   T. Evoking feelings of repulsion

KEY: VOCABULARY WORKSHEETS - *Poe Stories*

Worksheet 1	Worksheet 2
1. C	1. N
2. C	2. A
3. D	3. I
4. A	4. T
5. D	5. B
6. A	6. P
7. A	7. S
8. C	8. Q
9. A	9. C
10. D	10. F
11. A	11. H
12. B	12. J
13. B	13. D
14. C	14. K
15. A	15. M
16. D	16. O
17. D	17. G
18. C	18. L
19. C	19. R
20. C	20. E

VOCABULARY JUGGLE LETTER REVIEW GAME CLUES - *Poe Stories*

SCRAMBLED	WORD	CLUE
DIMA	AMID	In the middle of
NHTLIAANIE	ANNIHILATE	To reduce to nonexistence; to nullify or render void; abolish
PRANIOAPIT	APPARITION	A ghostly figure
NRESTAICA	ASCERTAIN	To find out
TETUSA	ASTUTE	Shrewd
SDUREAN	ASUNDER	Into separate parts or pieces
YDACUATI	AUDACITY	Boldness; daring
GEGULIBIN	BEGUILING	Deceiving; diverting
GZITAOCNN	COGNIZANT	Aware; familiar with
DENOCVICE	CONCEIVED	To form or develop in the mind; devise
SNEDIGOCN	CONSIGNED	Handed over
BROOOETARCSR	CORROBORATES	To strengthen or support with other evidence
TNUENASCOCNE	COUNTENANCES	Faces
VOTEECD	COVETED	Wished for longingly
BAPLLCUE	CULPABLE	Responsible; at fault
RSONIDEI	DERISION	Scoffing; ridicule
ISMINATOLUIDS	DISSIMULATION	Concealing one's true feelings or intentions
STIACECT	ECSTATIC	Euphoric; blissful
EGSUIGORE	EGREGIOUS	Bad or offensive
SEGSRE	EGRESS	Exit; escape
MAEDROEN	ENAMORED	Inspired; captivated
OCHPE	EPOCH	Age; time
PMEDIED	IMPEDED	Obstructed
PTUYINIM	IMPUNITY	Exemption from punishment, penalty, or harm
RCBEOLAVERI	IRREVOCABLE	Can't be turned back
VIIDL	LIVID	Bruised
CULDI	LUCID	Easily understood; sane or rational
VLENCLEEMAO	MALEVOLENCE	Ill will toward others; rancor; malice; evil influence, especially supernatural
FANDLOIM	MANIFOLD	One of many kinds
MNIE	MIEN	Manner
LBUNESOU	NEBULOUS	Cloudy, misty, or hazy
DOOSIU	ODIOUS	Evoking feelings of repulsion
BROS	ORBS	Eyes
LALIPD	PALLID	Pale; dull

Poe Stories Vocabulary Juggle Letter Review Game Clues Continued

SESESENERVPR	PERVERSENESS	Quality of being directed away from what is right or good; an appalling action, situation or object
ROIUISODPG	PRODIGIOUS	Enormous
OMPUUSLCISRYO	PROMISCUOUSLY	Casually; randomly
EQEIMUR	REQUIEM	A hymn, composition, or service for the dead
CSAGSAOUI	SAGACIOUS	Wise
CYAGSATI	SAGACITY	The quality of being discerning, sound in judgment
REES	SERE	Withered; dry
LUBMIES	SUBLIME	Majestic; inspiring awe; impressive
CBMDEUUCS	SUCCUMBED	Gave in
TNESIRLSSU	SULTRINESS	Sensualness; voluptuousness
RNUDVIEECEP	UNPERCEIVED	Unnoticed
DXEVE	VEXED	To bring distress or suffering to; plague
YACORVIT	VORACITY	Wild hunger

www.ingramcontent.com/pod-product-compliance
Lightning Source LLC
Chambersburg PA
CBHW051407070526
44584CB00023B/3327